Elevate Your Emotional Intelligence

Elevate Your Emotional Intelligence

A Parable That Reveals the Path to Better Relationships and a Happier Life

KATHY STODDARD TORREY

DISCLAIMER NOTICE:
This book is a work of fiction. The main character Maria is a life and leadership coach like the author. The things that Maria teaches are concepts that the author teaches in her workshops and seminars. Many of her personal examples are from the author's life. However, in the story Maria is dead so obviously not the author.

The other characters are made up and not based on real people. The main character John is an avatar for the perfect coaching client. He is open-minded and catches onto the concepts quickly. The characters have the mindsets and challenges common in many of the author's clients. Any resemblance to actual people, living or dead, or actual events (other than Maria's examples) is purely coincidental.

ISBN 979-8-9901826-0-8 (print)
ISBN 979-8-9901826-1-5 (ebook)

CREDITS:
Production Management: Weaving Influence
Cover and Interior Design by Maureen Forys, Happenstance Type-O-Rama
Copy Editor: Nick Wilbourn
Proofreader: Katrina Horlbeck Olsen

To my sons,
Nathaniel and Andrew.

From infancy to fatherhood, your presence in my life has been a journey of joy, challenges, and growth. From looking for bugs under rocks to profound philosophical discussions, you nudge me outside my comfort zone. Your resilience, kindness, and support have been the foundation of my own personal development.

Forever proud,
Mom

CONTENTS

CONTENTS

INTRODUCTION

THERE ARE LOTS OF BOOKS defining emotional intelligence and stating why it is important. However, there aren't many that give practical steps that a person can take to improve their emotional intelligence.

This book will help you to know yourself better, determine what's important to you and why, and create a decision ruler to make logical decisions and plans in alignment with your values and goals. It will also show you how to communicate clearly and create positive relationships at work and home.

If you read the book and do the exercises at the end of each chapter, you will gain an understanding of yourself and demystify the words and actions of others. Life will feel easier, and you will feel more confident.

The book is written in an easy-to-follow story format with lots of examples and stories that illustrate some complex concepts. One of the main characters uses a simple five-step method to go from rock bottom to recreate relationships with his children, coworkers, and boss. In the end, he has a foundation of peace and a feeling of flow in his life.

This book accomplishes all of those things by providing a road map to increase emotional intelligence. In its absolutely simplest form, emotional intelligence is broken down into four categories outlined in the following diagram.

	AWARENESS	MANAGEMENT
SELF	self-awareness	self-discipline
OTHERS	relationship awareness	relationship management

Self-awareness is the first piece of emotional intelligence to master, and it means that we have a realistic view of ourselves and our abilities. I know from coaching and training that getting an accurate picture of ourselves is harder than it sounds.

The first step in being self-aware is identifying our values and priorities. We can't make good decisions for ourselves if we don't ensure those decisions are in alignment with what is important to us.

The second step to self-awareness is knowing what topics and actions annoy us or make us angry; those are our triggers. Our triggers have more to do with our experiences and values than they do with other people. It's important to ask ourselves why they are triggers.

We start with self-awareness and learn our values, priorities, beliefs, and triggers. Then we move on to self-discipline.

Self-discipline means controlling our impulses; we pause to think before we act. In general, we want to avoid any behavior that doesn't get us closer to our ideal self. That could mean resisting a cupcake, controlling our temper, or doing our homework.

Our first impulse might be to yell at someone who has done a poor job or insulted us. However, yelling doesn't create a positive work environment or positive relationships.

Relationship awareness includes being aware of others' feelings and perspectives and taking an active interest in their concerns. Another big part of relationship awareness is anticipating, recognizing, and meeting the needs of others. It means being savvy about the politics around you, which means noticing and understanding a group's emotional currents and power relationships.

How can we do all that? It comes down to paying attention to the verbal and nonverbal cues of others, but especially the nonverbal ones. Nonverbal communication includes tone of voice, facial expression, and body language. When we pay attention to those things, we get a lot of information about what people are thinking and feeling.

Relationship management includes leadership skills that are often taught in leadership workshops. When we talk about relationship management, we are talking about things like coaching for improvement, motivating employees, and effective communication techniques. These are tools that leaders use to manage relationships.

The effectiveness of the relationship management tools depends on the foundation built by the other parts of emotional intelligence: self-awareness, self-discipline, and relationship awareness. It's important to work through the first three pieces of emotional intelligence, and end with relationship management. We can't "manage" relationships without mastering the first three parts.

The five-step program outlined in the book to increase emotional intelligence only works if you apply the steps and do the work. Like physical exercise, change only happens if you determinedly work on it consistently. At the end of the book, there is a link to download a checklist that will help you stay on track.

Let's see how John creates a life of ease and peace by using the Positive Effect Leadership 5-Step Method to achieve emotional intelligence.

THE STORY BEGINS

MARIA WAS RUNNING, and she was feeling frustrated. She usually enjoyed listening to the leaves crunching under her feet and the feel of the sun on her skin, but today those things were lost to her. Her ponytail swished back and forth, and a few strands of gray and dark brown came loose and stuck to her sweaty neck.

She was a life and leadership coach whose life was not going as well as she wanted—or expected. Her relationship with her husband was becoming more and more contentious, and she wasn't sure what to do about it. So far, none of her training or experience had helped. *Life coach, heal thyself*, she thought as she rolled her eyes. She helped other people create and strengthen relationships but couldn't seem to affect her own. The irony wasn't lost on her.

As she passed her usual halfway mark at the neighborhood playground, she began to feel a burning sensation in her chest. She slowed down to a walk. Another super annoying part of life, aging, was slowing her down. In her youth, she could run for several miles, but right now she could barely catch her breath. It felt like several things were slipping out of her hands.

As if to punctuate her point, the pain in her chest became intense, and she fell to her knees. Maria didn't understand what was happening. She felt her body hit the pavement, and the ringing in her ears drowned out the sounds of children playing. Then everything went dark.

She was dimly aware of things happening around her. The sound of an ambulance siren came closer. Someone lifted her onto a stretcher. There was an oxygen mask on her face, and then she was in a hospital room. Lots of machines were beeping. She couldn't move. Everything was foggy and surreal. People came in and out of the room, and she couldn't tell how much time had passed.

She opened her eyes and focused hard. She could see her children surrounding her. She saw the beautiful face of her oldest child, Emmy, that was so like her own. Emmy's face wore a look of devastation she didn't understand. Emmy's husband, Ian, was standing behind her with his hand on her shoulder. His face had a look of deep concern.

Antonio, her middle child, was sitting next to his sister and looking lost and forlorn. Antonio had her husband's green eyes and his odd sense of humor. Antonio looked up at his wife, Sanya, who was standing beside him. Sanya pushed a strand of Antonio's sandy hair away from his face. Then she took Antonio's hand and gave it a kiss. That made Maria happy. She liked this young woman.

Her youngest child, Russel, was sitting on her bed and holding her hand. His girlfriend, Tamara, stood behind him with her hands on his shoulders, supporting him physically and emotionally. Russel was talking and smiling at her, but she saw the tears falling from his crystal blue eyes.

She was filled with enormous love for them all. Then she wondered where her husband was. She felt a bit panicked. *Where is John?* She spotted him standing a bit apart from the rest. His sandy hair was messy, and he looked a little disheveled. His face looked sad and a little guilty. Despite their problems, she loved him, too. As she thought about the life and family that they created together, she felt an enormous satisfaction at having a life well-lived.

And then everything became foggier, and her perspective changed. Now, she saw herself from above. She thought that she looked old and frail—very different from the person who left home for a quick run. Suddenly, the room became a flurry of activity. Nurses and doctors were doing things she didn't understand, and her family watched in stunned silence.

The scene before her suddenly transformed to a memorial service. A parade of friends and family passed by. She saw former clients who she had helped transform their lives. They looked almost as sad and stricken as her family. One by one, family and friends told stories about her, shared happy memories, or talked about something she said to them that changed their lives. She had loved the movie *It's a Wonderful Life*, and this felt like a glimpse into the world without her.

It felt like she was there, but she wasn't really. It's like a dream—or maybe a nightmare, she thought. There were so many things she still wanted to do and say but now she would never have the chance. She would never be able to repair her relationship with her husband—never be able to tell him how much their life together had meant to her. She saw him sitting at the end of the family's row, staring off into space with a blank expression.

And then, before she could take everything in, the scene around her shifted once again. She felt like she was waking up from a very restful nap. She found herself standing next to her oldest child, Emmy, who was sleeping next to her husband. Her face looked less troubled than it had been before, but the occasional shifting and subtle flinches she made in her sleep made Maria think that maybe Emmy wasn't sleeping peacefully.

She tried to brush Emmy's dark hair from her face, but instead of making contact with warm flesh, her hand touched air. Maria looked at her hands in confusion, then tried again. Her hands would not make contact. She tried to lift the covers up over her firstborn but couldn't grasp them either. She heaved a sigh and realized that she was merely an observer in the world now.

She walked into the room of her two young grand-children, Grace and Luis. She wanted to pick them up and give them a grandma hug but instead just watched them sleep for a while. Then she thought about her other children.

She closed her eyes and thought of Antonio. She remem-bered his quirky sense of humor and warm bear hugs. With eyes still closed, she relived the last hug that he gave her. If she thought hard enough, she could feel the warmth that radiated from him and the clean smell of the soap he'd been using since he was a teenager.

When she opened her eyes, she found herself standing next to Antonio's bed. He and his wife, Sanya, were sleep-ing. They both looked peaceful and were lovingly snuggled together. They didn't have children yet, and she thought about how dearly she loved them both. They would make great parents.

Then she wanted to see her youngest child, Russel. Russel was 25 and not married, but she had always thought his girlfriend, Tamara, was a good match for him. She felt a wave of sadness as she realized that she wouldn't be a part of their wedding. She closed her eyes and thought of her baby. Russell was serious and intense, but very loving. He was also scrupulously honest and forthright. She thought about how she loved to watch his blue eyes when he talked passionately about his current topic of interest. She opened her eyes and found herself standing next to a sleeping Russel and Tamara. She was startled by Tamara's beauty even when she was sleeping. She was glad that Russel was not on his own. He probably missed her the most and showed it the least.

Then she thought of her husband, John. Their marriage had been on rocky ground lately. There had been fights and harsh words in the last year or so. She often went out for a run to escape the tension in the house. Running. She had been running when this bad dream started. Then, it finally dawned on her that she was probably dead. Had she died running? *Well,* she thought, *I escaped the tension and arguing, but death wasn't the solution that I had in mind.*

She wanted to see John. He had been her rock for decades before things started falling apart. She closed her eyes and thought of her husband at the beginning of their relationship. She remembered his mischievous smile, generosity, and general sense of fun. He was giving and thoughtful. She opened her eyes and expected to be next to her husband. After all, it had worked when she thought of the children. But she wasn't with her husband. She was still standing by Russel's bed.

She took a deep breath and closed her eyes again. This time she thought of the man her husband had become. He was short-tempered and angry at the world. She couldn't remember the last time he had smiled at her or the children, or the last time he had given her a truly warm hug. When their children called, he wouldn't answer the phone.

When asked a question, his answers were gruff, and any help or encouragement was given grudgingly.

She opened her eyes and saw her husband in front of her. He was not asleep like the others but sitting on the edge of the bed with his head in his hands. He smelled terrible, and she was surprised that she could smell things. She thought he might have been drinking and that he looked desolate.

Without thinking, Maria reached out and touched John's arm. She connected with warm skin, and he started. His head jerked upright, and his bleary eyes tried to focus on her. His sudden reaction startled her, and she stepped back.

As his eyes came into focus, recognition spread across his face, then disbelief, then a bit of horror. He knew what he was seeing, but his mind knew that it was impossible.

"John? Can you see me?" Maria asked, tentatively looking at him, as confused as he was in her presence.

He shook his head and said, "No, I cannot. I am imagining you. I wished you gone, and now my conscience is getting even."

Maria doubted for a moment that he had a conscience anymore and realized that her sometimes snarky inner dialogue had stayed with her in death. She seldom said the unkind or sarcastic things that she thought. She'd developed enough self-discipline over the years to keep her unhelpful comments to herself. Her husband, not so much lately.

Instead, she said, "I don't know how, but I am here. I am also not sure why I am here. I've seen the kids but couldn't touch them. They look good. You, on the other hand, can feel my touch and look terrible."

John seemed resigned to the insanity of the situation as he shook his head in disbelief. He sighed and said more to himself, "Great, a dead wife who is still around criticizing me." He went back to holding his head in his hands as if that would block her out.

Maria hadn't thought that her statement of fact was criticism, but it wasn't uncommon for him to hear something different than she'd intended. As someone who gave a lot of workshops on communication and emotional intelligence, Maria knew John was in Negative Sentiment Override towards her. Everything she did was further proof that she was a terrible person. In that state, he was incapable of seeing 50% of the nice things that she did, and he took offense at almost anything she said. It was a contributing factor to the downfall of their relationship.

She took a deep breath and said, "I apologize. It wasn't meant as a criticism. You look like you're having a rough time, and I'm concerned." She spoke as calmly and positively as she could. Using self-control in difficult situations wasn't any easier when you were dead.

John looked at her and said, "I thought my life would be better without you, but that hasn't turned out to be true. As it turns out, not everything wrong in my life was your fault."

In her head, she thought, *Well, I'm certainly sorry that my death wasn't the easy fix that you were looking for.* But she didn't say it out loud. She was annoyed and a little angry that he glossed over her death so easily. However, escalating the conversation into an argument wasn't going to be helpful at this moment.

She recognized that this was a major revelation for him and a big step forward in his self-development. Many of her clients began their journey believing that everyone and anyone else was to blame for their problems. After a few months of coaching, they slowly admitted that many of their problems originated within themselves.

"That's a major revelation and a lot to take in. I can imagine that it might be causing you to question a lot of things in your life," she said, feeling herself kicking into coaching mode.

"Yes, Hallucination," John answered. "It is. I must have absorbed more of your coachy mumbo jumbo than I thought."

Her being a hallucination made as much sense as anything else at the moment, so she decided to play along. She might as well be useful while she was present but dead. He'd probably be more open to ideas that he thought were coming from his own subconscious than ones that were coming from the wife he had grown to dislike.

"Well, you might as well use some of that coachy mumbo jumbo that's stuck in your head to help yourself. You are definitely not happy or well. Are you ready to change?" She used her coaching voice, the one filled with authority and confidence. Maybe she was here to help John get his life on track and find happiness, which she knew would also improve her children's lives.

John surprised her when he stood up and said, "Yes, I am. Your death really brought my own mortality home to me. I don't want to die knowing my children and grandchildren don't like me—don't really know me. And I've realized that I don't really know them."

He paced back and forth a bit and said, "I've let the people down at work a lot recently. I think they would have fired me if you hadn't died. Their sympathy will keep me safe for a while longer, but I want to rebuild those relationships as well."

John stopped for a moment, searching for words. Finally, he said, "I want to be the man I was when we got married.

I was happy and positive. I remember feeling a deep love for all three kids when they were born. How did I lose that? Now we have nothing to say to each other." Maria sat quietly, letting him continue his moment of self-discovery.

After a few minutes, he looked at her, and his eyes were filled with determination. He said, "I want to get my life back on track. I want to be a good father and a good friend." His strong voice trailed off for a second as he lowered his voice and gave a little shrug. "But I don't know how. I don't know where to start. I don't know if it's even possible."

In full-blown coaching mode and fueled by determination, Maria looked back at him and said, "I do. And you can do it in five steps."

GETTING READY

THE FIVE STEPS came clearly into Maria's mind. They contained the basic concepts that she'd been teaching for almost 20 years, but they were organized in a new way that made total sense. She could see them clearly written on a whiteboard in her own handwriting. It was nice to know that her mind was sharp even though she was dead.

"I can really turn my life around in five steps?" John asked hopefully as he rubbed his palms on the front of his shirt like he was trying to smooth out his wrinkled clothes.

"Yes," Maria replied, a small smile tugging at her lips. "You can create a peaceful life with positive relationships, but it will take some work." She stopped to let him absorb that, wanting him to understand that this is something he must want—something he must choose to work towards.

"There is one concept that you should be familiar with before we get started," Maria said. As soon as she said it, she realized that she had just "shoulded" on John. "Should-ing on people" was a phrase she used in workshops that usually got a small laugh from the participants. She tried to avoid telling people what they "should" do according to her perspective and encouraged everyone else to do the same.

So she rephrased the statement and said, "There is one concept and one object that will help you move through the steps more quickly. You are already familiar with the object."

John looked puzzled, and she smiled and said, "Let's start with that."

Power of Choice

Understanding the concept that she had in mind required a shift in mindset for many people. It was a foundational leadership principle. *Well*, she thought, *It's really a foundational principle that makes decisions and life easier.*

"Although it doesn't always feel like it," she said to John, "we do always have the power to influence what's going on in our lives." She paused to think about how she could demonstrate her point, then said, "Let's do a short exercise that I do in leadership workshops. In the end, you will become reacquainted with an object that I know you are familiar with."

She smiled a little mischievously and said, "Grab a pen and paper."

Maria waited as John stood up to get something to write on and something to write with. When he looked back at her with a pen and paper in hand, she continued, "I'm going to start a sentence and you finish it with as many things as you can think of in one minute." John sat down at the desk and Maria said, "Finish the sentence 'I have to . . .' with as many things as you can think of. I will give you a minute to make a list."

John raised an eyebrow. Maria thought that there might be some pushback, but he surprised her when he nodded his head and started writing.

John came up with the following list:

- Get out of bed in the morning
- Get dressed
- Drink coffee
- Go to work
- Water the plants
- Go to the grocery store
- Pay taxes
- Talk to people
- Clean the house

Maria saw that he had several things on the list and stopped him. "Okay," she said, "Now I'm going to change the sentence to 'I choose to . . .'. Do the things on your list still make sense?"

John read over his list and said, "Some of them still make sense. I guess I choose to water the plants because I've chosen to keep the plants. I'm not sure about the rest."

Maria asked him for an example of something he felt that he had to do, and he said, "Pay taxes."

"You do choose to pay taxes. You could choose not to pay taxes and go to jail or hope that you didn't get caught. You are choosing the course of action you think best," Maria explained.

"Okay," John said and nodded, "but I have to eat to live, so I have to go to the grocery store." He stood up looking at the list in his hand.

Maria smiled and admitted, "You do have to eat if you want to live. However, you can get your groceries delivered or subscribe to one of those boxed meal services and get them in the mail. You could also eat out at every single meal. You do have choices about how you get your food to eat."

"Okay," John said, mirroring her smile as a look of understanding crossed his face. "I get it. I could quit my job and stop drinking coffee. Work and coffee are choices that I'm making."

"That's right!" Maria exclaimed. "We do have to eat, sleep, and breathe in order to keep living. However, most everything else is a choice. Life right now, for the most part, is the result of the choices we've made up to this point. People in my workshops usually groan at that statement. It is true, and it hits home. We have made some really good choices in our lives and some not-so-great choices that have led us to our current situations."

John immediately said, "I didn't choose to become a widower. I didn't choose to suddenly live alone."

"Very true," Maria said, softening her tone a bit. "You didn't choose that. However, you do still have some choices."

"What's important to note," she continued, "is that our future is determined by the choices that we make now. We make choices all the time without thinking about how they will affect the future. The key is to make choices intentionally—both about what we do and what we think.

"We must decide where we want to go, what we want to accomplish, and who we want to be. I call choosing with intention 'waving around the Magic Wand of Destiny.'" Maria paused after her long explanation and waited for John's reaction.

John was well-acquainted with the Magic Wand of Destiny. Maria had created an actual magic wand that she took with her when she presented workshops. He'd once delivered it to Maria when she'd forgotten it. In fact, the Magic Wand of Destiny was still in her office, standing in a vase. He hadn't had time to clear out her things yet. He corrected himself—he hadn't chosen to clear out her office yet.

Maria was still talking, "Choosing on purpose creates a completely different way of looking at the world. It can change what you do, and it can also change how you think about what you do."

John was already thinking about things like clearing out Maria's office differently, but he wanted some more examples. "How so?" he asked as he put the paper and pen back onto the table.

"When I first did the exercise of completing the sentence 'I have to . . .,' I wrote that I had to make the kids' breakfast and lunch every morning. I didn't really like making breakfast and lunch, and I would lie in bed in the morning groaning to myself about it."

John remembered seeing Maria every morning in the kitchen fixing breakfast and lunch for the kids as he was leaving. This happened all the way through the kids' high school days. She never seemed resentful about it.

Unaware of John's temporary trip down memory lane, Maria continued, "However, I liked chatting with them in the morning and wanted to ensure that they had good food to eat. Getting up and fixing meals were actions that were in alignment with my values. That realization didn't change what I did, but it changed how I felt about doing it. When I woke up and thought, 'I have to . . .,' I stopped myself and started waving around the Magic Wand of Destiny. I told myself to either get up and cheerfully fix food or stay in bed. The kids were in middle school and capable of fixing their own food if I had chosen not to do it."

That was a revelation of sorts for John. She'd chosen to do something cheerfully. It was a concept that had never occurred to him before.

She briefly stopped as a memory came back to her, then smiled and said, "When I started working again, I hired the cleaning service because I didn't want to clean the house anymore."

"You had other choices," John interrupted. "You could have made the kids and me clean some of the time."

Maria looked at her husband skeptically and said, "You are right. I did have other choices. *And* 'making' you guys do it felt like an even bigger challenge that I decided to avoid while starting a new job." She'd done air quotes with her fingers when she'd said "making."

John realized that he and the kids had resisted many of her requests for help around the house. As the stay-at-home mom for a while, she'd taken on most of the household chores. He didn't see it at the time, but now he saw that she'd kept most of those chores when she'd started back to work, and that hadn't been fair.

Maria was talking again, unusually unaware that her student was having an epiphany. "In life, we have three choices in most situations. If we don't like what's going on, the first option is to try and change it. If we control the situation, it's easy to change. If we have no control, then changing it isn't an option. In most situations, we have some influence that we can try to exert.

"Do you remember when we were in Oklahoma and Antonio was having trouble breathing at school?" she asked him.

John did remember. Antonio had asthma when he was young and was allergic to dogs. One of the other students had a helping dog, and the school would not keep Antonio and the dog apart. It had gotten to the point that they had quadrupled Antonio's asthma medication. "We went in and talked to the school about the dog," John said.

"Yes," she agreed. "We didn't completely control the situation, but we did have some influence. We met with teachers and the principal. I sent them information on asthma and allergies."

"Didn't you give them straws and have them breathe through those after jumping up and down?" John asked, a smile playing on his lips.

"Yes, I did," Maria said unapologetically. Then she shrugged her shoulders and said, "But it was all to no avail. They did not cooperate. We were unable to change the situation.

"Our second choice was to accept the situation. Acceptance means to truly accept the situation, not grit your teeth and endure it. Accepting means making a mental or physical adjustment that you can live with that won't stress you out. In our case, we were already quadrupling Antonio's asthma medicine, so we couldn't really accept the situation."

"We ended up putting him in that private school until he got out of middle school," John added.

"Yes," Maria said. "The third and final option is to flee. Fleeing doesn't have to be a negative event. You can plan ahead and leave a situation on good terms. It turned out well for Antonio. He did really well at the private school. He wasn't Emmy and Russel's brother there. He got to create his own identity.

"It's important as we move through the five steps that you realize that you can choose to make changes along the way. The power of choice is," she paused searching for the right word, "well, powerful!"

She continued, "Nothing changes if you don't believe that it can." She waited a second and then said, "You cannot change your life, your circumstances, or yourself unless you intentionally choose to do so."

Your Turn

You read about John beginning his emotional intelligence journey, and now it's your turn to start your own journey! The power of choice is a foundational concept for personal development and change. Here is a summary of what John learned in Getting Ready along with an exercise that you can do.

It would be a good idea to start these exercises in a notebook or binder so you can look back over them whenever you want to. There will be a list of things for you to try and practice at the end of each section.

- **Power of choice.** Most of us have more power over our lives than we realize. It's easy to get into a victim mentality and feel that we are stuck without any choices. We say, "Oh, I have to do this" and "I have to do that." In reality, most of the things that we do are choices.

  John made a list of things that finished the sentence, "I have to . . ." Even with the foresight you've already gained, it can be an interesting exercise. Without thinking too much, complete the sentence, "I have to . . ." with as many things as you can in about a minute.

  Now, look at the list and ask yourself which ones are choices. Then ask yourself which ones are really choices that you want to continue to make. For example, if you wrote that you have to water the plants to keep them alive, do you want to keep the plants and the responsibility of watering them?

What's important to note is that our future is determined by the choices that we make now. We make choices all the time without thinking about how those choices will affect the future. The key is to make choices intentionally.

Summary

Before you try to change any behavior, it's crucial that you believe that you have the ability to do so. Embracing the power of choice in your life moves you from a victim mindset where you "have" to do things to a more empowering way of looking at life.

✓ Without thinking too much, complete the sentence "I have to . . ." with as many things as you can in about a minute. Now look at the list and ask yourself which ones are really choices. Then ask yourself which ones are choices that you want to continue to make.

STEP 1:
——————— KNOW YOURSELF ———————

SHE LOOKED AT JOHN and said, "The first step is pretty easy. We can do it right now if you are ready."

She looked at John and noticed that there was a bit of excitement in his eyes. He sat up straight but said casually, "Sure, Hallucination. Why not?" He was working to act like he didn't really care.

Maria had seen this with clients many times. In the beginning, they didn't want to be vulnerable and display their despair and hope openly. She knew it was a defense mechanism, and she also knew that it was temporary. She'd gotten past this barrier many times before—as long as the person truly wanted their lives to change. She'd told John about the power of choice and the Magic Wand of Destiny. It was time to see how serious John was about using it to change himself and his life.

Values

"OK," Maria said with enough enthusiasm for the both of them. "Let's say that you died suddenly," she went on, putting the emphasis on "you" and smiling at him. After all, she had just died suddenly. She then asked, "How do you want to be remembered? What do you want people to say about you at your memorial service?"

John stood up and began walking around the room. He said, "I've actually given this a lot of thought lately. People said a surprising number of good things about you at your memorial service. I had no idea that you had such a positive effect on so many people's lives. Some of them flew in from far away to tell the story of how you helped them at a major turning point in their lives."

The word "surprising" stung Maria a bit, but she was gratified to learn that her work as a coach and human had helped others and been appreciated. She turned her attention back to John.

He sat back down on the bed and said, "Right now, I don't think anyone would have many positive things to say about me." It was a difficult thing for anyone to admit but an important first step for John. One can't change what one can't see or acknowledge.

Maria sat down next to him on the bed and asked gently, "How do you want to be remembered?"

He thought for a moment before he said, "I want the kids to say I was a good father."

"What sorts of things would a good father do?" Maria asked. She was prompting him to describe his vision of a "good father."

John sighed, looked at his phone on the dresser, and said, "Well, to start with, a good father would answer the phone when one of his children called."

She smiled and said, "That's a good start. What else?" She wanted him to come up with a more detailed description.

"I would listen to them, too," he said with more confidence and a stronger voice. "They would know that I cared." He paused to think for a moment. She could tell that he was replaying in his head some of his recent interactions with their children.

He continued, "They would feel confident that when I said something, I meant it and I would do what I said I would do." Maria suspected that these were things that John had not been doing. There was also a good chance that he was behaving the same way with other people besides the kids.

Maria said, "So, if we translate those into qualities that you want to embody, I heard caring, trustworthy, and dependable. Do those sound right to you?"

"Yes," he said with a little more excitement. "I also want to be more positive and less grumpy." Then he took a deep breath and said, "It's exhausting to be angry all the time. I want to let that go." He thought about Maria's original question and said, "'Angry all the time' is not something I want to be remembered for."

"That's really good noticing and self-awareness," Maria said proudly. "Is there anything else?"

"I was really taken with how much you helped people." He turned to look at her, and she saw a clear note of sincerity in his blue eyes that looked just like their youngest son's eyes. "You made a positive difference in many people's lives. I would like to have the same positive effect," John said in a very determined and matter-of-fact voice.

Maria smiled back at him in acknowledgment of his kind words. Mentally, she was grateful that Step 5 had appeared in her head and knew they would talk more about the value of helping others then. "That is an awesome list," she said. "Let's write it down so we don't lose any of those values that you want to embody."

John got up and walked to the desk. He picked back up the paper and pen, then wrote down the words *caring*, *trustworthy,* and *dependable*. Then he paused to consider how to describe making a difference in people's lives. He put the end of the pencil in his mouth in a gesture that Maria was very familiar with. He always did that when he was thinking. After a moment, he decided to write *helpful.*

He showed Maria the list, and she said, "Those are really great." She remembered him saying that he didn't want to be grumpy and angry anymore and asked, "Do you want to add positive?"

John nodded and added *Be positive* to the list.

Maria continued, "This is a list of your values. You can use the list as a decision ruler for any actions that you take. If you are considering saying or doing something, pause and ask yourself if you'd be acting in alignment with these qualities."

Values
_____

caring
trustworthy
dependable
helpful
Be positive

John read through the list. He did want people to remember him as having these values. He put the list next to his phone on the dresser, where he would be sure to see it the next time the phone rang.

Priorities

"Next," Maria said as she got up, "It's a good idea to clearly define your priorities. We can only have three as our main focus at any one time. Let's get a snapshot of what is important to you right now."

She decided to do the exercise with sticky notes like she did in her workshops. She had seen sticky notes on the desk earlier when John was rummaging around for a pen and paper. "I'm going to tell you a list of possible priorities one at a time. Write down each priority on a sticky note and stick it to the desk."

She cleared a space on the desk by pushing some papers aside. Interestingly, she could move objects when she was in John's presence. It was weird but not any weirder than anything else going on, so she just accepted it.

She clearly remembered the list of priorities that she had called out for years during leadership workshops. "The first one is career or job. Which word do you like better?" She pulled off a sticky note and handed it to John.

John paused in thought, then bent down to write down *job*. "I feel it's a little late in life to think about career progression, but job fits." He shrugged as he showed her the sticky note.

"Great," Maria said as she pulled off another sticky note and handed it to him. "The next one is finances or money. Which do you like better?"

"Making money is related to my job, so I think I will go with finances, which would include investments and money management." John's practical brain was firing on all cylinders, and he enjoyed the feeling of being focused.

"That's good," Maria said, enjoying how engaged John was. "Now, which is more important to you: finances or job?"

"I think job is more important right now," John said after some thought.

"Then put the sticky note with finances under the sticky with job on it," Maria said as she pointed towards the cleared desk. Once John was done, she continued, "Let's go on. You will reorder the stickies as needed each time I list a new priority."

They slowly did the same procedure for the rest of the list of priorities:

- Community/Friends
- Creativity/Hobbies
- Altruism/Volunteering
- Health/Fitness
- Food
- Personal Development/Professional Learning
- Leisure Time/Fun
- Family (close and/or extended)
- Significant Other/Romance
- Spirituality/Faith

Once they'd gone through the list, she asked if he could think of any others. He stopped to think. When nothing came to mind, she continued, "Well, what are the top three stickies? What do you want to focus on right now?"

John turned back to the desk with the numerous sticky notes, and Maria noticed that romance was at the absolute bottom. Oddly enough, she felt relieved.

"Family is at the top," he said as he pointed at the sticky note with *family* written in big, bold letters. "I feel like they need me now. Your absence has been a big blow to them. I feel like I can help and make a difference in their lives right now."

Maria badly wanted to say "thank you" and give him a huge hug, but she didn't want to overwhelm him. She was so frustrated that she couldn't help her children and their families anymore. It was a comfort to know that he was willing to make them a priority right now. She decided to tell him.

"I am grateful that you are putting family first right now. Profoundly grateful," she said as her own brown eyes teared up a bit.

He looked a bit embarrassed and said, "It's okay, Hallucination. I'm happy to help." He continued before she could respond or acknowledge his words, "I think that job should be the next priority because I'm probably in danger of losing mine."

She knew he was changing the subject to avoid dealing with strong emotions. She also hoped that, at the end of the five steps, he wouldn't avoid talking about feelings—his and other people's.

"That's very practical and astute," Maria said, changing subjects with him. She immediately pulled herself together and went back into workshop mode. "And the last one?"

"I think it is going to be *health*. I've been eating poorly and drinking too much alcohol." He took a deep breath and said, "I just don't want to be here. I don't mean *here* in this room or city or state." He spread his arms out gesturing around the room. "I don't want to be present in life. It's too hard. It feels like there is too much to overcome."

She put her hand firmly on his shoulder to remind him that he wasn't alone. "You are facing a lot," she acknowledged. "It will be an uphill battle, but the view from the top will be magnificent." She smiled encouragingly at him.

John looked up at her and said, "Thanks. I think it's easier when you don't have to go through it alone, Hallucination."

Well, that's progress, she thought. John had shut most people out of his life for the past few years and had been going on his own for the most part. Her smile broadened, and she said, "I think that you are right."

At that moment, his phone rang on the dresser. The shrill sound made them both jump. John picked up the phone and looked at the screen. "It's Emmy," he said.

She wasn't surprised. Emmy was their oldest and a typical oldest child. She checked on everyone to make sure they were okay. She organized family events and kept everyone connected. Of course, she was checking on her father.

Maria could see her calling her dad while chopping veggies for dinner or folding clothes. She often called while she was doing household chores. Maria had enjoyed these phone calls with Emmy. They got to visit for as long as it took Emmy to complete tasks.

John started to put the phone down, but Maria said, "Up, up, up, up, up! You just said that you were going to start answering their calls." She pointed at the list of values John had placed next to his phone.

John looked at her with furrowed eyebrows, then looked back at the phone. He took a deep breath, accepted the call, and said hello. John looked like someone was about to force him to take foul-tasting medicine.

Maria could hear the surprise in Emmy's voice when she said, "Dad!" Emmy was too emotionally intelligent to say, *I'm surprised that you picked up*, though Maria was pretty sure that's what she was thinking.

John put a smile on his face and said, "Hey, baby girl!" He looked at the word *family* on the top sticky note on the desk.

She could imagine Emmy's eyes rolling at this diminutive and slightly insulting greeting. John was tone-deaf to the way his comments grated on Emmy's nerves. She was a grown woman with a career, a husband, and two children. She was not a baby girl. Being more aware of how he affected other people was another thing that could change during Maria's five-step program for John.

Maria picked up John's list of values off the dresser and handed it to him. She wanted him to remember the kind of person and father that he wanted to be:

- Caring
- Trustworthy
- Dependable
- Helpful
- Be Positive

John read over the list. He paused for a beat and then said, "What can I do for you?" There was a pause. Maria knew it was because this was a question that Emmy wasn't used to hearing. She could imagine a bit of confusion on her daughter's face. John usually responded to questions but didn't ask many. And an offer of help right off the bat was pretty unusual.

"Actually," Emmy said slowly, "I was calling to see how you are doing—to see what you are doing."

John looked at Maria. She could see that he was considering saying, "I'm talking to a hallucination that looks a lot like your mother." They had been married for a long time before she died, and she could read his expressions.

Instead, John took a breath and said, "I'm working on pulling myself together. I'm sorry that I haven't been there for you, Antonio, and Russel. I know that losing your mom so suddenly has been difficult for all of you."

Maria was impressed. John was starting to live his list of values right away! She took it as a sign that he was truly ready to start changing his life for the better.

There was a stretch of silence, and Maria could hear Emmy sniff. She imagined Emmy holding back tears that she refused to let fall. In Emmy's world, crying was a sign of weakness. Emmy finally choked out, "Thanks, Dad. That's sweet," she paused for a second, before adding, "I've missed you."

Maria thought that John might not be the only person to change during their work on the five-step process. That often happened with her clients. They couldn't make other people change, but by changing their own behavior, they invited change in others. Many times, that invitation was accepted by her clients' friends, family, and coworkers.

Now, it was John's turn to choke up. "I've missed you, too," he said in a voice that was a little hoarser than usual. He got a hold of himself and said, "How are Grace and Luis?"

"They are good," answered Emmy, laughing nervously. Maria thought that she was relieved to be back on familiar and factual footing. Before John could ask, she continued, "Ian is also doing well."

Ian was her husband of eight years. They had met at a networking event soon after they graduated from college and hadn't been apart for very long since then. Maria liked Ian. She liked the respectful and loving way he spoke with Emmy. Ian was also kind and fair with the children. She was grateful and happy that Emmy had Ian.

"In fact," Emmy went on, "I was calling to ask you to dinner this weekend." Emmy's voice sounded a bit formal. She was making an offer that she didn't expect to be accepted. Maria thought it felt obligatory.

Immediately, John tensed up. Maria could see him coming up with excuses not to attend, so she quickly pointed to the sticky notes on the desk. Specifically, she picked up the one on the top of the column of stickies that said *family*.

John sighed, gave Maria a look of mock exasperation, and said, "I would love to." His words sounded sincere.

Emmy was once again taken aback by an unexpected response. She stuttered as she said, "That's great! How about 5:30 p.m. on Saturday? We eat early so we can get the kids to bed at a decent hour and have some time for grown-up talk."

"That sounds good," John said with a smile, and he sounded like he meant it.

Maria realized as her shoulders relaxed that she had been quite tense during their conversation. In life, she had been the go-between in conversations involving John and her children. It was a responsibility born of fear. Family harmony meant a lot to her and she was constantly protecting it. As she reflected on that, she also realized that it hadn't been necessary or helpful for the health of the family's relationships.

John hung up and looked at Maria. "Well, that wasn't as hard as I thought it would be." As he thought about dinner at Emmy's, he said, "However, I do have to go to dinner now and make polite conversation. You know that I don't always see eye-to-eye with Emmy." He looked a little worried at the prospect of a lengthy conversation.

"It will be fine," Maria said. "We can do a little prep that will make the night go easier for you."

Frame of Reference

"It will be fine," Maria assured John. Then she thought for a minute and said, "And it would help a bit if we had a conversation about our Frames of Reference and triggers before you go."

"What do you mean by Frame of Reference?" John asked as he placed his phone back on the dresser.

Maria took the pen and paper and drew a picture of the Frame of Reference, as she had many times on a whiteboard at the front of a classroom or lecture hall. It felt good to be putting her knowledge and expertise to good use right now to help her family.

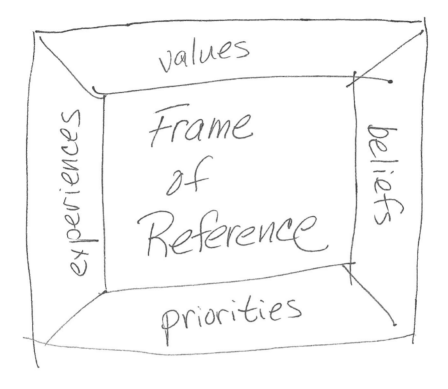

Maria gave John a moment to look at her drawing before she began to explain, "Our Frame of Reference is made up of four parts: values, priorities, experiences, and beliefs. We've already talked about your values and clearly defined them." She pointed to where John had placed his list of values. "We've also discussed your priorities, and you've picked your top three," she said as she pointed to the sticky notes on the desk.

As they both reviewed the list of priorities, Maria remembered to tell John something important. "By the way, putting a priority at the bottom of the list doesn't mean that it's not important to you at all; it's just not something you focus on right now. Remember, this is a snapshot."

She went back to sit on the bed before continuing with her example, "When the kids were young, family was at the top of my list. Once they were grown, I started focusing on my career. Family was at the bottom of my list, but that didn't mean that I didn't love them or think they were important. I just wasn't spending as much time or energy on them."

She thought with a little guilt that "significant other" had slipped down her list of priorities over the years as well.

She shook her head to get back to the present with John and said, "The third part of our Frame of Reference is experiences. The things that happen in our lives have a profound effect on how we view the world and experience life in the future. For example," she said, gesturing with her hands, "You know the story of me wanting to be the fire marshal in elementary school."

John looked at her quizzically. He obviously didn't remember the story. Maria sighed and continued, "The fire marshal made sure that the windows were closed, left the room last, and turned the lights out. I wanted to be the fire marshal, but girls weren't allowed to be the fire marshal back then."

John sat next to her, listening to her story. She continued, "At first, the principal told me that I couldn't be the fire marshal because my long hair was a fire hazard; if the room was on fire and I was the last one to leave, then my shoulder-length hair was more likely to catch fire than a boy's shorter hair. At that time, all boys had short hair cut over their ears and cropped close up the back."

John smiled knowingly at his wife and said with a grin, "I imagine that you didn't accept that answer."

"No," Maria laughed, "I told the principal that I would cut my hair like a boy so that I could be the fire marshal. At that point, he rolled his eyes and mumbled something like, 'Don't be a problem, Maria. You cannot be the fire marshal.' Then, he told me to leave his office."

She shook her head at the memory before continuing. "That experience, coupled with several others about what I wasn't allowed to do because I was female, made me very sensitive to chauvinism and any sort of discrimination. When I look at the world through my Frame of Reference, assumptions based on gender appear to be surrounded by fire with a big neon arrow pointing at them. I don't miss one, and I'm indignant and angry about all of them."

Maria thought for a moment and said, "I think that Emmy sees the world in a similar way." Maria could picture Emmy's indignant expression as she bolted through the door relating a story of some insulting comment or ridiculous assumption that someone made. Maria sighed, because even if the world had changed some since her own childhood, it was not enough to please Emmy and herself.

She came out of her reverie about Emmy and continued, "I've learned not to react and overreact over the years, but the noticing and the feeling are still there." It had actually taken a lot of practice to improve her self-discipline and ensure that her thoughts didn't immediately run out of her mouth. "I see a different world than a person who isn't fussed about stereotypes and equality."

She looked at John and asked, "Do you have any experiences that shape the way you view the world?" She could usually predict John's answers, but she wasn't sure what his answer was going to be to this question.

John thought for a minute, and Maria waited quietly for an answer. Another exercise in self-discipline, but she'd learned a long time ago how to sit comfortably in silence to let someone think.

John sat and thought for a moment. Lately, he seemed to notice every wrong in the world around him. More specifically, it seemed that most of the wrongs were aimed at him. He realized that he expected them and looked for them through his Frame of Reference.

He looked at Maria as if remembering she was there. He said, "I feel like I'm always on the lookout for people to say insulting or disrespectful things." He took a deep breath and continued, "If I look at the experiences that led me to look for insults, it probably stems from my father who was big on not allowing people to put him down. He'd say, 'You can't let people piss on your pride.'" Maria looked at him with confusion, and he explained, "I think today he would say, 'Don't let anyone disrespect you.'"

Maria knew that there was a lot of insecurity present when someone felt that they were being insulted constantly by innocuous remarks, and she knew her father-in-law had not grown up in a supportive environment. It all made sense to her.

"That's very good noticing," Maria said. "The first step is realizing we have a tendency to react in a certain way to certain things. Then we get to decide if we want to change. We'll talk more about that later."

Maria went on to explain the last part of the Frame of Reference. "Over time, our experiences create our beliefs about ourselves and life in general. Beliefs are the final part of our Frame of Reference. Many of them are the foundations of our lives—personal rules that we don't realize exist.

"For example, I see many people who are hesitant to draw, sculpt, or write. Somewhere along the way, someone criticized one of their creations, and they created this belief about themselves: I can't draw. When I do draw, it's embarrassing."

She went on, "When we are young, we mess up and don't do things perfectly, which results in the 'I can't do anything right' belief. A series of disappointments at the hands of others can create the victim's belief that 'bad things always happen to me.'"

Maria switched from the doom-and-gloom side of beliefs and said, "Beliefs can be positive as well. I took drama lessons for eight years starting in first grade. I had a lot of positive experiences being up in front of people. My belief is that 'I do a good job in front of a group.' I also believe that 'I am not less capable or intelligent because I am female.'

"That belief is interesting because it's the opposite of what I often heard growing up. If I'd just taken my experiences to heart, then I'd be convinced that being female made you less capable and intelligent."

Maria paused. She'd done a lot of talking. She shrugged and said, "Our Frames of Reference create the world that we live in. If we believe good comes to us and we have values and priorities that foster positivity, then we might have a sparkly bright Frame of Reference that helps us to see the good in the world. Intentionally examining and creating our Frame of Reference can make all the difference in the life that we experience."

Maria's words were swirling through John's mind. He felt caught in a loop of negative thoughts. Out loud he admitted, "I think my Frame of Reference is a heavy black frame lately."

Maria couldn't argue with that assessment because she felt that John's view of the world had been negative and dark for the past few years.

She said, "You can change it if you want to."

John looked at her and said, "How do I change the way I see the world?" It seemed like an impossible task to him.

Noticing the Good

Maria knew it was possible to change the way one sees the world. She had seen her clients do it, and she had done it herself.

She began, "Humans naturally notice the problems and dangers around them. Back in the days of the cave dwellers, the humans that were on the lookout for saber-toothed tigers outlived the ones who nonchalantly meandered through the meadow." She thought of how different—and stressful—her life had been when she sought out negative things to comment on.

"Today," Maria continued, "we still look for problems to solve and things to fix. We get in trouble with our parents and bosses if we don't. Because most of us don't like to get into trouble, we are constantly looking for things that might cause a problem."

"So," John said, "it's a sort of hopeless situation."

"Not at all!" exclaimed Maria. "Just because we tend to do something a certain way doesn't mean that we are doomed to follow that tendency. We can make some intentional choices to do things differently." John looked unconvinced.

Maria remembered an exercise that she did in work-shops and decided to do it with John. "Notice all of the red things in the room," she said as she pointed around them.

John's eyebrows lifted in doubt, but Maria smiled at him in encouragement. He looked around and mentally made note of the red book, the sleeve of a red shirt sticking out of the closet, and the red flowers in a painting that hung on the wall. He hadn't liked the painting much when Maria bought it, but since her death he'd become fond of it.

Once his eyes stopped wandering around the room, Maria said, "Now close your eyes." John obliged and she said, "Tell me about the blue things in the room."

John laughed as he opened his eyes and said, "I have no idea!"

Maria laughed, too. It felt good to laugh with John again. "Of course not!" she said. "Because that's not what you were intentionally noticing. The first step in becoming more pos-itive is intentionally noticing the good things around you."

John's smile faded a bit, and he asked, "What sorts of good things are you talking about?" Maria could tell clearly that he didn't think that there were many good things around him.

"Well," she said, "we could start with the fact that you are alive." She made a gesture to herself with a smile and a shrug.

John laughed again and rolled his eyes, "Okay," he said, "Being alive is good."

"In the beginning, start with the basics," Maria told John, getting back to the topic at hand. "You have a warm place to sleep, running water, indoor bathroom facilities, a job, a nice car, and a family."

John looked skeptical. "Those aren't great things," he said.

"But they are good things," Maria emphasized. "Being grateful for what we have is the first step in improving our outlook on the world." She looked at him and asked with genuine curiosity, "What are you grateful for?" Once again, she was reminded that she didn't know her husband as well as she thought because she wasn't sure of what his answer would be.

John thought for a moment. What was he grateful for? Lately, he'd spent all his time thinking about what he was missing in life or what had gone wrong. He could readily list at the end of the day every instance when someone had been rude or every detail that had not gone his way. He'd also been dwelling on the choices he'd made in life that had led to outcomes he didn't like. He was mad, for instance, that no one had helped him make better college degree and career choices.

"Hmmm," John said while he was thinking. "I am grateful for the kids. I'm grateful that Emmy checks on everyone and keeps the family together. I'm grateful that Antonio has found Sanya. They seem to have so much fun together. I'm grateful that Russel followed his talent and became a carpenter." He was proud of his children, too, though he wasn't sure that it was something he said often.

"I'm grateful that we were able to help Russel launch his carpentry business." Maria added. They had given him a good start in his business and helped create the success that Maria was very grateful for. Russel earned a good living doing something he liked.

John looked at her and said, "That's right! We did. I'd forgotten that."

"Do you remember 'Carpentry Christmas' when we all gave him tools for Christmas?" Maria asked, the memory washing over her. She remembered Russel's surprise when he opened Maria's gift. The entire family had given him some kind of carpentry tool, but Maria had given him a beautiful tool box that was large enough to hold most of his other presents.

Russel had been so excited and grateful to receive most of the tools that he needed to get started. Maria could still see the surprise and joy that had been on his face as he unwrapped each present.

"I do," John said, his eyes looking far away. "I learned a lot about calipers, clamps, and jigs that Christmas." He sat for a moment fondly reminiscing about family holidays gone by.

The small smile on John's face told Maria that he was getting lost inside a good memory. That was good. Remembering good times was a great way to rekindle positive emotions, so she let him enjoy his memories.

She sat with John and remembered her own family memories. She thought of her mom, who was one of the most positive people that she had known. Maria's mom was referred to as Grandma Laura because Maria had taken the title of Grandma.

John was fond of Grandma Laura, and Maria remembered the gratitude journal that her mother kept for years. At the end of each day, Grandma Laura would write down three to five things that happened during the day that she was grateful for.

Maria asked, "Do you remember the gratitude journal that my mom kept?"

John nodded and said, "I remember her journals. We read through them after she died. There were lots of great family memories recorded there."

Grandma Laura was good at capturing small moments in her days. She wrote about things like getting a hug from her husband and petting a puppy. She also documented things that she did with her grandchildren, like reading books and going for walks. As John thought about it, her gratitude lists rarely included grand gestures and vacations. The entries were mostly about small moments that had made his mother-in-law happy.

Maria broke into his thoughts. "A gratitude journal can be a great way to become more positive. We scan our days for things that we can write about in the evening. This helps to train our brains to look for the positive things that happen each day.

"And if we are feeling profound gratitude, we can't feel any other emotion. It's a great way to keep our minds from spinning as we go to bed. If you don't want to keep a journal, you could just go over the positive moments of the day when you get into bed at night."

John had once again begun reminiscing and roused himself out of his thoughts of the past. "I think I could start with that," said John. "I don't think I'm ready for a gratitude journal just yet."

"Fair enough," said Maria. "There is only one more thing that we need to talk about before you have dinner with Emmy."

"What's that?" asked John who seemed to be genuinely interested in what she had to say.

It is lovely to be listened to, thought Maria. She realized that neither of them had sat down and genuinely listened to the other for quite some time. A wave of regret washed over her.

Triggers

"What's the last thing?" John asked, bringing her out of her reverie.

"Oh, sorry," Maria said, shaking her head to clear the memories. "It's triggers."

"What is a trigger?" John asked, resigned to learning about one more thing.

"Triggers are usually things that challenge our values or beliefs," recited Maria as she settled back into workshop mode.

John looked at her with more skepticism than understanding, so she chose a different approach. "Okay," she said, "You know that I react to the word *ladies*. I don't like it at all."

John nodded, "I know that, but I've never really understood why." He looked at her curiously, waiting for a response.

In her head, Maria thought, *That's because you've never really cared to listen and find out,* but she didn't say it out loud. Another win for self-discipline. If she voiced her resentment, they would get off track.

Instead, she said, "Our values and beliefs are often based on our experiences. I just told you the fire marshal story, so you know I'm sensitive about anything having to do with gender stereotypes."

John got a little testy, rolling his eyes as he said, "But *lady* is just a word to describe a group of women, like 'ladies and gentlemen.'" He said "ladies and gentlemen" like an announcer in an arena, standing with his arms open wide, which only served to annoy her further.

"That's true," Maria said calmly, recentering herself and remembering that the outcome of helping John would not be achieved if she rose to his verbal bait. "And I'm not arguing with that statement. However, it has an emotional charge for me because I was told to 'sit down and be a young lady' when I was young. It meant stop running around, stop arguing, stop speaking your mind, stop questioning authority, stop being loud, stop having fun." She ticked off the list on her fingers as she spoke.

Maria's voice had risen, and her tone was a little angry. She said the phrases the same way that she'd heard them as a child. She took a breath and continued, "The implied message was, 'Young ladies sit still. Young ladies are quiet. Young ladies sit around looking demure and smiling a lot.'"

John's eyes widened at Maria's intensity. "I can see why you wouldn't like doing that," he said with an apologetic smile. He thought of how often he had called Emmy a "young lady" and briefly wondered if she had the same sentiments about the phrase as her mother.

She smiled back at him and replied, "I really wasn't good at those things and resented feeling that the only way to be accepted and lovable was to be a young lady in that sense."

John stopped and thought for a moment, trying to think of his intentions when he said the word "lady." He thought of it as a respectful term. He thought that most people probably felt the same way, so he said to Maria gently, "Not everyone who uses the word 'lady' is trying to insult you or make you angry. Most people don't see the word the way you do."

"Absolutely true!" exclaimed Maria. The force of her answer startled John. She raised her arms in the air and said, "That's the point! It's my trigger. It has little to do with anyone else but me. It's important that I recognize that and not get mad or upset when anyone uses the word. It's my issue to deal with."

Maria's words made sense to him because, from his perspective, he knew he wasn't trying to offend anyone when he used words they might find triggering. It made him wonder about what things he was taking offense to that weren't intended to be offensive by the person speaking. "How do I know what my triggers are?" John asked Maria.

"One of the best ways to figure it out is to determine where you spend your emotional energy," Maria said. "Think of emotional energy as Emotional Pennies. The first step in determining our triggers is to pay attention to how we are spending our Emotional Pennies." She stopped when John didn't look like he was following her train of thought. She took a different approach and said, "Think of the things that upset you and make you angry."

The thoughts about triggers had already been going through his mind, so John started thinking about the things that made him angry or upset. It didn't take long. He already knew what upset him and made him angry. The top thing on his list was how much he hated it when people questioned his authority, plans, or answers.

He also knew what experience led him to feel that way. He thought about being grilled mercilessly by his father about any ideas or plans. Then his father would do his best to shoot them down and belittle him.

Maria knew he was thinking about things that triggered him, because it was evident by his clenched fists and the angry expression on his face. She said gently, "Things that make us angry are usually our triggers, and we spend a lot of Emotional Pennies on them."

Maria started pacing and gesturing like she was in front of a group. "Let's say that we each have 100 Emotional Pennies to spend each day," Maria said. "The goal is to have as many Emotional Pennies as possible at the end of the day, and you can't carry any over to the next day."

"Why does it matter if I have any Emotional Pennies left at the end of the day?" John asked a bit aggressively. He was still carrying some anger from the memory of his father. He heard the aggressive tone of his own voice and tagged a smile on the end of his question.

The effect was that he looked like a snarling dog, but she recognized the effort and smiled back. "After a day of work, do you feel tired or energized when you get home?" Maria asked.

"I'm usually exhausted," John replied immediately. He didn't have to think about that one.

"And are you tired because you did a lot of physical labor during the day?" Maria asked.

"No," John replied with a bit of sarcasm. The answer was obvious. She knew he worked in an office. "I'm mostly tired from dealing with people and problems." Just a few days ago, he had to intervene when a coworker was being disrespectful to a client. Once that was done, he joined a meeting where one person was talking over everyone else and refusing to listen. Then he started to work on a report that was long overdue. All this happened before lunch. He'd used a lot of Emotional Pennies that morning.

"Exactly," Maria said with a smile. "You've used up all your emotional energy, or we can say you've spent all your Emotional Pennies. By evening, you only have energy to sit in front of the TV and veg out."

John nodded his head in agreement. "That's true," he said. "Most nights I barely have enough oomph to fix dinner."

"Yes," Maria agreed. "So, we want to identify where all our Emotional Pennies are going. One of the easiest expenditures to get rid of is the one that we throw at our triggers."

She continued with an example. "If I tossed a handful of Emotional Pennies every time I heard the word 'lady,' I'd have spent them all by the end of the day."

"Are triggers the only thing that we spend Emotional Pennies on?" John asked. He was thinking of a few things that he felt were genuinely important to him. He didn't think he was being triggered when he stood up for an idea that would help his clients and the organization.

"No," Maria answered as she picked up a pile of clothes from her favorite chair in the corner of the room and sat down. She put the clothes on the floor and said, "Some common things that we all spend emotional energy on are work, family, health, other people's problems, spirituality, friends, and things over which we have no control. Your list may not have all of these items and probably has quite a few more."

She tucked her feet up under her and said, "The key is to figure out which of these are wise investments, and which are wastes of our Emotional Pennies. Triggers are the first thing to deal with and get rid of, but we make unwise expenditures of our Emotional Pennies on other things as well."

Maria stopped to see if John had any questions before she continued. He seemed to be following along, so she went on, "A totally silly way to spend Emotional Pennies is on things over which we have no control. My personal pet peeve is when someone gets angry or cross for days when their favorite professional team loses. Tying your sense of well-being and happiness to a group of people you do not know and over whom you have no control seems about as absurd as being angry over which direction the wind is coming from."

This was a familiar one, John thought. On more than a handful of occasions, he found himself yelling at the TV during Philadelphia Eagles games. He was even louder when he watched the games with his friends as everyone fed on one another's energy. He did toss some Emotional Pennies at the TV during games, but he didn't hang on to any anger or frustration after the game, unlike two of his friends he had grown up with. They were unbearable to be around for a week or so after the Eagles lost. He felt like it was a good sign that he didn't carry the anger and frustration around for days.

Maria continued her leadership workshop lecture after a short pause to let John process her words. "The first step in limiting our unnecessary expenditures of emotional energy is to pay attention to how we are spending our Emotional Pennies. In everyday life, we want to invest our emotional energy in things we enjoy, people we love, and situations that we can change for the better. A good test question to ask is: If I face this situation and invest some emotional energy into it, can I resolve it so that I never have to put another Emotional Penny into it again? If the answer is yes, then go for it! Break off the relationship, improve the situation, and/or release that old resentment."

She looked at John and shrugged, "As a general rule, you want to avoid any situation that constantly drains your emotional energy with no hope of the situation improving or resolving."

"Like triggers," said John. He thought to himself, *I'm never going to get people to stop questioning my plans and ideas.* Out loud he said, "You are never going to get the world to stop using the word 'lady.'" Just as he recognized that he couldn't stop people from questioning what he had to say, Maria couldn't stop people from using the word that triggered her.

"Very true," said Maria with a smile. "All I can do is choose not to be upset." Clearly, John now understood the concept of triggers and Emotional Pennies—that the point wasn't to control other people, but rather oneself.

"Emotional Pennies are a great tool to help us put the moments of our day to best use. We can dramatically improve the quality of our lives by spending our Emotional Pennies with intention. By spending them on things that give us a return investment in love, support, and satisfaction, we can create a life that doesn't exhaust us," said Maria.

John sighed as the words washed over him. He now understood that his irritation with people questioning him was his issue to deal with and not the fault of everyone around him who had a right to ask for explanations. Maybe they were just interested in his thought process. He asked people questions all the time because he wanted to understand their logic or reasoning. Yet when the same was done to him, he took it as a challenge and would often react inappropriately.

"You make it sound easy—you just choose," he said, shaking his head. He didn't think it would be that simple. Even with all the information he had now and the awareness he'd gained about why he reacted the way he did to certain things, it would still be hard not to take things personally.

"Well," Maria said with a gentle smile, "it's simple but not always easy. I still flinch a bit when someone calls me a lady, but I've worked on it a lot, and it gets easier. I remind myself that they aren't intentionally insulting me or implying that I need to behave myself. Those thoughts are translations that happen when the word goes through my Frame of Reference."

With renewed energy, Maria said, "Now, let's get back to the present. Can you think of anything that Emmy says or does that triggers you?" she asked John.

John thought for a moment before he said, "Yes, she is always suggesting things for me to do like I'm a child. And she does jump on her soapbox now and again about that environmental stuff."

"Why do those things bother you?" Maria asked. She refrained from saying, *Emmy isn't the only one who likes to tell people what to do.* She could remember several instances of receiving unwanted micromanaging from John over the years. Instead of speaking, she let John figure it out on his own.

John's thoughts mirrored Maria's. Once he thought about it, it was sort of silly to get mad at Emmy for doing the same thing to him that he often did to her. He promised himself that he would accept all suggestions gracefully. He might not follow through on them, but he would listen and say thank you. He did remember Maria saying that feedback is a gift and saying thank you is the appropriate response.

Maria watched him think for quite some time. He sort of shook his head, and she thought he'd had some sort of revelation. She'd thrown a lot of information at him, so instead of insisting on an answer to her question, she said, "That's the end of Step 1."

"That was a lot of information for one step," John said grumpily, running a hand through his disheveled hair as he moved back to sit on the bed.

Maria smiled. He'd done amazingly well in some pretty strange circumstances. "Yes, it is," she said, "but it all has to do with self-awareness—how well we know ourselves. Want a summary?"

John was tired and losing interest, but he was determined to change his life. He wasn't sure how long this hallucination was going to last, and he wanted to take advantage of it while he could. He took a deep breath. "Okay," he said. "Go for it."

She pointed to the Frame of Reference diagram again.

"Our Frame of Reference influences how we see the world, and it can also help us make good decisions. We want to do and say things that are in alignment with our values and priorities. Do you remember yours?" she asked.

"I remember that my priorities are family, job, and health," he said confidently, and she felt a twinge of pride. He was listening and remembering. He really was doing a remarkable job.

"That's awesome!" Maria said with a clap. "You are really doing a marvelous job at this stuff. Truly!" John looked a little embarrassed but was grateful for the acknowledgment.

"Now," Maria asked, "Do you remember your values? Think of who you want to be and how you want to show up in the world."

"Let's see," John contemplated. "I want to be more positive and less angry. I want to be a good father, which means I will listen to our kids and care about them. I'll also be dependable and trustworthy." He lifted a finger for every value he said.

Maria was looking at the list of values that John had written. What he said wasn't exactly the same, but as long as it had meaning to him, it didn't matter. There was one thing missing, though. "Would you want to make a positive impact on their lives?" Maria asked with raised eyebrows.

"Yes!" John said as he abruptly sat up straight. "The last one was to be helpful!"

Maria was honestly impressed with the work that John had done in the last hour or so. He'd done it with openness and sincerity, which were really good signs that he was ready to make real changes in his life.

"Our Frame of Reference can distort our reality a bit because we see things through the lens of our own experiences and beliefs. Most of the things that bother us, our triggers, are our own personal challenges and have little to do with other people."

Maria began to pace and talk enthusiastically, "We can free ourselves once we recognize what bothers us and why. We aren't stuck with our childhood beliefs. We can change them if they aren't supporting us." She stopped to make sure John was listening.

He was listening attentively, and she could see that he was fully engaged in this review.

"Finally," Maria continued, "keeping track of how we spend our Emotional Pennies is a great way to figure out what's draining us so we can make some changes. In every situation that we don't particularly care for, we have three choices: change, accept, or flee."

John added quickly, "And we can always wave around the Magic Wand of Destiny to make intentional choices. The one thing that we always have control over is how we think about a situation."

Maria didn't remember mentioning that specifically during their discussion, but it was true. Perhaps he'd absorbed more of her coachy mumbo jumbo, as John called it, than either of them had realized.

John stood up from the bed and said, "Thanks, Hallucination. I feel better. And I think I'm going to focus on my priority of health by taking a shower and eating some decent food."

"Excellent idea!" Maria said. She could still smell and wholeheartedly believed that a shower was an excellent idea.

Dinner at Emmy's

Dinner at Emmy's had gone reasonably well for John. He had accepted her health and wellness tips with grace. Every time she said something that he didn't agree with, he visualized her looking through her own Frame of Reference at the issue and at him. He was determined to spend as few Emotional Pennies as possible.

Emmy was meticulous and driven—a typical first child. However, she was kind and loving to her children, which John was happy to see. Ian wasn't treated quite as well, but he took it in stride. John watched him not take any of Emmy's comments, which John felt were slights, personally. Ian just accepted and loved her. It was kind of amazing to John.

Maria was there, of course, but no one knew. She stayed out of John's line of sight. She knew that her presence would make him feel judged and awkward. However, she wanted to know how the dinner was going and if he'd really taken his commitment to values and priorities seriously.

Eavesdropping wasn't exactly ethical, but were there rules for dead life coaches? She laughed at the absurdity of it all and decided that it was fine to give in to her curiosity about her husband dining with her daughter.

She was pleasantly surprised to see that John did not seem to take any of Emmy's comments about politics or the environment personally. She did see him take a couple of deep breaths, but on the whole, he did really well.

She asked him about it later, and he explained that he just kept imagining her talking through her Frame of Reference. This made her curious.

"What did her Frame of Reference look like to you?" she asked him.

John thought about it for a minute. He hadn't paid much attention to the picture frame that he made up for Emmy. "Now that you mention it, it was a rather odd-looking frame," John laughed. "It was pink and sparkly on the outside edge and the inside, with some shiny black thrown in. I think of Emmy as the little girl who loved to wear and own things that were pink and things that sparkled. She was such a cute little girl who loved her daddy."

John paused to remember Emmy in a pink, sparkly tutu twirling in front of him. "Watch, Daddy!" was a phrase he used to hear all the time. He remembered tossing her into the air while she giggled and whooped. He also remembered her small arms around his neck when she gave him a hug. Their relationship had been so easy then.

Maria interrupted his thoughts by asking, "What does the shiny black part represent?"

John thought about it for a second before he answered, "It's the adult she is now. More rigid and professional— also more reserved. The black part is like a wall that keeps her from showing the world too much of her sparkly pink nature." He looked at Maria, "I do think it's still in there."

"I do, too," Maria agreed. She was sad to think her daughter was reigning in her natural exuberance in order to be a responsible adult. Maybe she'd feel comfortable letting some of that pink sparkly stuff out in the future.

John added, "And I kept thinking, you aren't getting any of my Emotional Pennies for that!" And he laughed. Maria laughed, too. She was amazed at his progress. When someone is determined to change their lives for the better, the results are astounding. He was doing great.

Your Turn

Step 1 is all about knowing yourself, as the foundation of emotional intelligence is self-awareness. Here is a summary that includes some things that you can do to increase your self-awareness and develop your self-discipline muscle.

- **Values.** For the most part, our values stay the same throughout our lives. Our values are the first thing we need to consider when making a decision, since they create a decision ruler. We can ask ourselves, "Would this action be in alignment with my values?" If not, it's probably not a good idea.

   Picture your own memorial service in your head. You've led a full and meaningful life with which you are satisfied. What three things do you want people to say about you? What would you be very disappointed about if they didn't mention it?

   The list that you come up with is your values. Write them down and keep them close. Whenever you are feeling uncertain about something, pull out your list of values and ask yourself what you could do that would be in alignment with your values.

- **Priorities.** Our priorities change over time. It's a good idea to check in on them periodically. Priorities are another thing to consider when making a decision; they can be another part of our decision ruler. We can ask ourselves, "Would this action be in alignment with the priorities that I have right now?"

   Below is a list of possible priorities. Rank them from one to 12. Putting something at the bottom of the list doesn't mean that you don't care about it. It just means that you aren't spending a lot of time and energy on it right now.

  → Career/Job

  → Finances/Money

  → Community/Friends

  → Creativity/Hobbies

  → Altruism/Volunteering

  → Health/Fitness

  → Food

  → Personal Development/Professional Learning

  → Leisure Time/Fun

  → Family

  → Significant Other/Romance

  → Spirituality/Faith

Write down your top three priorities on the same paper or notebook as your values. Once you have checked in with your values, look at your current priorities for guidance on the best course of action.

- **Frame of Reference.** Along with values and priorities, our experiences and beliefs make up our Frame of Reference.

What we experience in our lives has a profound effect on how we view the world and experience life in the future. Over time, our experiences create our beliefs about ourselves and life in general. Many of them are childhood beliefs that become the foundation of our lives—personal rules that we don't realize exist. As adults, we get to examine our beliefs and decide if they are serving us well or not.

Uncovering our beliefs is the most difficult of the self-awareness exercises because we believe our beliefs to be true. We believe that we can't draw because some kid in third grade made fun of our drawing. We believe that we can't have successful relationships because some have failed in the past. However, we get to choose which beliefs we hang on to and which ones we let go of by pausing to examine them.

Make a list of the significant events in your life. Start with your earliest memories and go through to the present. Include both positive and negative events that have made you who you are. Write a short description of each event, and then write down the effect that it had on you.

For example, my mom told me that I had big ears when I was very young. I hid my ears for years! As an adult, I realized that I really didn't have big ears. It is possible that I misunderstood her all that time ago.

On the positive side, I took drama classes beginning in first grade and won a few drama competitions. As a result, I feel very confident when I'm up in front of people. You get the idea.

Look at each entry and decide if the belief you formed is supporting or limiting. If it's limiting, ask yourself if you need to keep it. Does the situation look different in hindsight?

The list of significant events can also uncover the sources of some triggers.

We can get rid of a lot of stress if we realize that the values, priorities, experiences, and beliefs of others are not identical to our own. Every person has a unique Frame of Reference that leads them to see things differently and make different decisions than the ones that we might make. We can accept that and know that *different* is not necessarily *wrong*. This realization makes life easier for everyone.

- **Noticing the good.** Human beings have a tendency to notice and remember the negative things that happen in life. However, we are not doomed to dwell on life's less-than-desirable events. We can choose intentionally to change our focus.

  As leaders, we want to develop positive relationships. In order to do that, we have to maintain a positivity ratio of at least 5:1. In other words, we must have about five positive interactions with a person for every negative interaction that we have.

To maintain a 5:1 ratio, we need to be noticing and commenting on what is going right all the time! It can be a challenge because leaders are trained to look for and comment on problems. However, research tells us that commenting positively and showing appreciation for a job well done is very motivating.

We can begin to create positive relationships by noticing what is going right both at work and at home. If we see someone doing something that we would like to see them do again, we should comment on it positively. We want to show gratitude for effort and action. The results are astounding!

Set an intention to notice one positive thing a day about three people in your life. They can be family, friends, or workmates. Keep it up for at least one month. By then it should feel less awkward, and you can start adding more people and more positive comments.

I did this with my sons when they were in high school. At first, they were suspicious of my motives. But after a while, they started making positive comments to others, too.

We are more likely to notice the good if we are in a positive frame of mind. Practicing gratitude is a powerful way to cultivate a positive outlook on life.

Keeping a gratitude journal can help us create a more positive frame of mind. Each day, write down a few things that you are grateful for. You can enhance your gratitude practice by thinking of all the small, positive interactions that you had with people during the day. (A smile and "hello" count!) Writing down what you are grateful for and reminding yourself of the small moments of positivity that you've had throughout the day can create a powerful spiral of positivity in your outlook on life.

Grandma Laura is my mom. She lived with me for 10 years, and she did keep a gratitude journal. She wrote down funny things my kids said and wrote about the happiness of hearing my sister's voice on the phone. We did read her journals after she died, and they were full of wonderful memories for us— and they helped her live a joyful life. She didn't start out that way, but she became one of the most positive people I've ever known.

- **Triggers.** Triggers are the things in life that set us off. Sometimes, we are triggered when something goes against our values. Other times, a trigger can be a reminder of an experience that upset us.

  Imagine that you have 100 Emotional Pennies to spend each day. You don't get to carry any over to the next day, but you want to end up with as many as possible. The more Emotional Pennies you have by bedtime, the more peaceful and energetic you will feel.

  Keep a log of the Emotional Pennies that you spend for a week. Are you wasting pennies on people or events that you can't change? Have you used all your Emotional Pennies on your drive to work? Awareness is the first step. Just notice where you are spending your emotional energy.

- **Decision Ruler.** We can't make good choices unless we know what we want to achieve. We must decide where we want to go, what we want to accomplish, and who we want to be. We also need to consider our values and priorities. Using those decisions as a guide, we intentionally choose actions, attitudes, and perspectives that move us closer to those goals.

Think about what you want to achieve in the next year that would get you closer to your life goals. Consider career, health, finances, and relationships. For each category, write down what you want to achieve in the next year.

Keep that paper with you. Put your values and priorities on it as well. You now have a decision ruler. Before you make a decision, look at your values, priorities, and goals. Ask yourself what action or mindset would be most helpful in this situation.

Summary

Here are the exercises to raise your self-awareness. Don't feel pressured to start them all at once. Choose the ones that look interesting to you right now. Once you complete one exercise and feel ready to move on, look at the list and pick the next one. Increasing your emotional intelligence is a lifelong journey.

- ✓ Determine your top three values by considering what you want people to say about you at your memorial service.
- ✓ Pick your top three priorities right now from this list:
  - Career/Job
  - Finances/Money
  - Community/Friends
  - Creativity/Hobbies

- Altruism/Volunteering
- Health/Fitness
- Food
- Personal Development/Professional Learning
- Leisure Time/Fun
- Family
- Significant Other/Romance
- Spirituality/Faith

✓ Make a list of your life-shaping events. Decide whether each experience created a supporting or limiting belief.

✓ Intentionally say one positive, supportive thing daily to three important people in your life for one month. Notice any changes in their behavior or mindset.

✓ Start a gratitude journal. Each day, write down a few things that you are grateful for. Before you go to sleep, think of all the small, positive interactions that you had with people during the day. (Again, a smile and "hello" count!)

✓ For one week, keep a log of your Emotional Penny expenditures. Notice which ones feel like a good use of your emotional energy. Look for patterns that can reveal your triggers.

✓ Think about what you want to achieve in the next year that would get you closer to your life goals. Consider career, health, finances, relationships, and who you want to be. For each category, write down what you want to achieve in the next year.

✓ Create your decision ruler. On a sheet of paper or index card, write down your values, priorities, and goals. Look at it each time you are making a decision that you feel uncertain about. Then, ask yourself what action or mindset would be most in alignment with what you want in life and who you want to be.

STEP 2:
———— DETERMINE THE ————
DESIRED OUTCOME

NOW JOHN WAS FACING another encounter that he wasn't looking forward to—a discussion with his boss, George.

"So, what is the meeting with George about?" Maria asked as John busied himself in the kitchen. She plopped down in her favorite chair in the living room. It was upholstered with a satiny fabric that always felt cool and smooth. She was glad that she could feel it even if John had to be around. *Still a little snarky,* she thought. Personal growth was an ongoing challenge even in death. She smirked at the thought.

She didn't really mind having him around and vowed to improve her mental discipline. *Love and acceptance. Love and acceptance. I'm only sending love and acceptance.* It was her new mantra whenever she started feeling less-than-positive feelings about someone. She might as well make use of her extended stay for her own personal development as well as John's.

"I'm not entirely sure, Hallucination, but I'd like to talk about it," John answered as he came back into the living room, a glass of water in hand. It was easier for him to believe he was talking to a hallucination than to his dead wife, which was a little alarming if he stopped to think about it. So, he didn't.

Desired Outcome

Maria was used to being called a hallucination now. She smiled and asked, "Well, what outcome do you want from the conversation?"

"I want it to go well!" John said a little too emphatically, as he sat down opposite Maria.

"Specifically, what do you want to happen during the conversation?" she prompted him.

John thought for a moment before he said, "I want to have a calm and reasonable discussion with George. Our discussions have been more like arguments lately."

Maria nodded in understanding before saying, "Developing and maintaining a positive relationship should be one of the goals of every discussion at work. It's the basis of professionalism." She added, "It's also a good goal in our personal lives, but let's focus on work for now."

She thought for a minute and said, "What would be a good way to begin the conversation?"

"With an apology," John answered immediately. "As I've been thinking about what I'm grateful for each evening, I've thought of George several times. He's been supportive and patient with me, even if he loses his temper and yells sometimes. I'd have lost my temper with me, too."

Maria was impressed with the observation and the fact that he had been doing the gratitude practice before going to sleep. She decided to tell him, "That's an awesome idea. I'm impressed."

John looked slightly embarrassed but before she could add anything else, he quickly went on. "I think he might want to talk about one project in particular that is behind schedule. This one is not my fault exactly. I mean, we aren't behind because I've been slacking off."

"So, what's going on?" Maria asked with genuine interest. She was intrigued. To her, business challenges were like a pile of yarn that needed to be untangled. The answers were there once you untied the knots.

John answered, "The main problem is that we need information from someone who is in another department. All I can do is ask nicely or yell and hope for the best. Neither has worked very well because we aren't high on this person's list of priorities. A poor performance for us doesn't hurt the person's overall job performance rating."

Maria had seen this challenge many times before when coaching clients. "That is frustrating," she emphasized. "What do you want George to do?"

"I want him to go to that guy's boss and report him. I'd really like him to go and pound on the guy's desk and frighten him. George can be a scary guy." John smirked, and Maria knew that wasn't what John really wanted.

"OK, having George take care of it is one possibility. Are there others? I think I asked a leading question when I asked what you wanted George to do. Really the outcome that you want is for that information to arrive on your desk when you need it. Right?"

"Yes," John said as he leaned back and plopped his feet onto the coffee table between them. He caught on pretty quickly to Maria's line of thinking. "Maybe George and I could brainstorm some solutions. For example, I might be able to get my hands on the raw data without waiting for the organized and pretty report. I don't need everything that is in the report the guy sends me."

What vs. How

"It's the *what* that's important, not the *how*," Maria said. John looked at her quizzically. "It's just what you said— what you need are certain pieces of raw data. That's the outcome that you want. How you get it is something that you can figure out with George. It's good not to go in with a set solution in your mind."

"Can you give me another coachy example, Hallucination?" asked John, a slight smile gracing his lips when he called Maria a hallucination.

The moniker "Hallucination" was beginning to feel like a term of endearment. She gave him a wry smile in return and said, "Sure."

She decided to use the example that she gave in workshops. "Let's say that you've been late to work regularly, and I want to talk to you about it. I believe that you just can't get yourself up in the morning so the outcome that I want is for you to get an alarm clock and put it on the other side of the room. I think that's the best outcome."

She paused to check if John was following along before she went on, "But there could be many reasons for you being late. Maybe one of your children is sick or your car is acting up. The outcome that I really want is for you to show up for work on time. How you manage to do that is something that we will figure out together during our discussion. Maybe some flex time is in order for a bit. There is no way of knowing what is best until we talk about it together."

"Okay," John said as he nodded his head in understanding. "I get it now. The 'what' is getting the data I need. The 'how' is something I will figure out with George, and it may or may not include roughing up the guy who sends me the report now." He smiled.

He was joking around, and she knew it. It was nice to see him lightening up a bit, looking more relaxed than she remembered him being in a long time.

"I do feel obligated to point out that roughing someone up is not appropriate workplace behavior," Maria answered as she smiled back at him.

"Point taken," John answered without any hint of malice or irritation, raising his glass towards her before he took a large sip.

Action Alignment

"There is one thing that I often see my clients do that I'd like to mention," Maria said. "It has to do with making sure that your—one's—actions are actually inviting the behavior that you want to see." Maria made the switch to the objective pronoun because she realized "your" sounded accusatory.

She then added, "We don't always act in a way that helps us get the outcome that we say we want."

"Is this something that I'm doing?" John asked with a frown as he put the glass down.

"It's something that we all do," Maria answered reassuringly. "I just want to mention it so you can be on the lookout. It's a trap that is especially easy to fall into when dealing with friends and family."

"Let's hear it," John said as he leaned back again, making himself comfortable on the sofa.

He looked so much better. He was less angry. His color was better, and he was keeping up with his health commitment. He'd even started going to the gym! She was proud of him and started to tell him, but decided to stay on topic right now since he seemed interested.

"The best way to explain it is with an example," Maria said. "Let's say that you regularly come home from work later than you say you are going to."

"I thought you said this was not something I did," John said in an amused tone as he raised an eyebrow.

"It's just a common example," she said as she shook her head at his teasing tone. "One of those things that I often heard about from frustrated clients."

Maria continued, "So we talk about you being late. I explain how frustrating it is to be given a certain time to plan around and then have you show up late. You explain that things happen at the last minute, but you will do your best to show up on time."

John said, "Sounds good so far to me."

Maria answered, "Yes. It was a good discussion. Let's say you come home ten minutes later than you said, and I've been stewing for ten minutes. However, it's much closer to your scheduled time than when you usually come home. You have obviously made an effort."

"Good for me!" John interjected good-naturedly, making Maria smile.

"I've said that the outcome that I want is for you to come home on time, but you didn't make it exactly. I can wave around my Magic Wand of Destiny and make an intentional choice. I can acknowledge your effort and thank you for trying, or I can give in to my irritation and say something like, 'Even when you try, you can't make it when you promise to.'"

"Ouch!" John touched his heart in an exaggerated manner like he had been wounded.

"Exactly!" Maria said, ignoring his antics but happy he was engaging. "Which response is more likely to motivate you to try harder in the future?"

"The first one would definitely be more motivating," John said. Then he made a keen observation. "I can see how much more satisfying it would be to feel righteously right and dress down the person."

"Exactly," Maria said again. "It feels good at that moment to vent your frustration, but the feeling of satisfaction doesn't last, *and* it doesn't invite the behavior we really want. It just continues the struggle. All we get out of it is continuing to be right as the other person is totally unmotivated to meet our desires and expectations."

She let her words hang in the air as John processed them before asking, "Do you feel ready to talk with George?"

"I do," John said with a confident smile. "I think it's going to go well. George is a reasonable guy even if he is rough around the edges."

And just as John had predicted, the conversation did go well. Maria eavesdropped again, but this time she had John's permission. John started with an apology and told George that he was grateful for George's patience and understanding. That opening statement started the conversation out on a positive note.

John clearly laid out the challenges with the project and specifically talked about the challenge of getting all the information that he needed. John explained that one particular person was in charge of creating a report with information that John needed, but he was missing the monthly deadline and—by extension—causing John to miss his deadlines.

John and George discussed various options and then came up with a creative way to get the information that John needed in a timely manner. George asked the person who provided the one piece of information John needed to send it to John when they sent it to the guy creating the report. John would no longer have to wait for the entire report to be created, which meant he could hit his own deadlines and move his project forward. The guy who created the report was out of the loop, along with a lot of frustration.

As Maria listened to George and John chatting after they'd agreed on a solution to get the outcome that they wanted, she thought about the next step in her plan and wondered what would happen when they finished Step 5.

Your Turn

In Step 2, you learned about the importance of knowing what you want to achieve at the end of a conversation. You also read about what to focus on during the conversation in order to get that outcome.

- **Desired outcome.** Before we begin any conversation, we must be clear about what we want to get out of it. In other words, we must define our desired outcome. One outcome we always want is to create or maintain the positivity of our relationship with the other person or people.

- **What vs. How.** Defining our desired outcome can be tricky. We usually want to define *what* we want to happen but leave *how* it will happen to be decided in the discussion.

Before you start a conversation, think about what you want to achieve. Be careful to define the outcome in terms of what, not how. Remember, how the outcome will be achieved is something that will be determined during the conversation. Avoid going in with set solutions in your mind.

- **Action alignment.** How we react to a person or situation can greatly influence the outcome that we get. There is a lot of momentary satisfaction in yelling or making snide comments when we are upset. However, those types of actions don't get us to the outcome that we want.

  Before you say or do something, especially when you are upset, ask yourself what action would best get the outcome that you want. Many times, our egos want immediate satisfaction when we feel our pride has been hurt or someone is taking advantage of us. Always keep your desired outcome in mind, and make sure your actions are ones that will help you reach it.

Summary

The things to do for this step happen when you are interacting with other people. These exercises will be much easier if you've completed all the exercises in Step 1. Self-awareness is an essential component of self-discipline, which is required in Step 2. You can't get to your desired outcome if you can't strategically control what you say and do.

✓ Before you begin a conversation, clearly define the problem and the outcome that you desire.

✓ Remember to focus on what you want to happen, not how you want it to happen.

✓ When you are upset, always consider your desired outcome before you speak or act. Ask yourself what actions, words, and attitudes would give you the best chance at achieving your desired outcome.

STEP 3:
———— READ THE ROOM ————

JOHN HAD ALWAYS gotten along well with Antonio because they were both fun-loving goofballs. They enjoyed the same movies and had the same sense of humor. However, he did not have the same easy relationship with Russel. Their youngest child was serious and determined. Russel had more in common with Emmy than Antonio, even though they were both males and closer in age. John never understood Russel and didn't realize just how off their relationship really was. Russel dreaded talking with John, but John didn't know this.

Russel had invited John to go to dinner with him and Tamara. John didn't see anything weird about this since his relationship with Emmy had improved, but Maria thought that something was up. She thought that Russel was going to talk about getting married. Maybe Tamara was pregnant? Maria did pop in to see her children and their families now and then but tried to respect their privacy. She was tempted to hang around Russel to figure out what was going on but decided against it. She would hear about it when John did, same as if she were alive.

In preparation for dinner with Russel and Tamara, Maria thought it was time for Step 3 of her five-step plan.

She turned to John and asked, "Are you ready for Step 3, which is 'Read the Room?'"

John looked startled and said, "I thought we were done. Everything is going much better. I feel better."

Maria agreed with him. Things were going better. Much better than she had hoped, in fact. But he still had some room for improvement. He still wasn't catching all the clues that people were giving about what was going on and how they really felt. John was better, but he still had little awareness of how other people were doing.

"I agree, and I'm happy you feel better about everything so far," Maria said. "And there are still some things we can work on that will make it better."

John was feeling a little stubborn and said, "I think I have everything under control."

Johari Window

Maria decided that it was time to talk about the Johari Window. "Let's go out in the backyard and sit down for a minute. It's a perfect evening out there." John followed her out a little grudgingly.

They sat in the comfy Adirondack chairs on the patio. Maria had always liked sitting here. Without fail, the evening breeze hit her perfectly from this spot, and the shade from the pin oak tree she planted decades ago felt protective.

Once John was settled, Maria asked, "Do you ever remember me talking about the Johari Window?" she asked.

"No," John said, his deep voice sounding a bit like a growl. "And I'm not sure I want to."

The tone made her feel defensive, but she took a breath and centered herself. After all, she was dead. What's the worst thing that could happen?

She turned to John and said earnestly, "Please indulge me. I am still here, and I'm hoping it's for a purpose. Do you mind letting me try to fulfill it?"

John contemplated for a second, let out a long sigh, then reluctantly said, "Fine. I was just hoping that all the self-improvement stuff was over."

"Truly, John, it's never over!" Maria let out a small laugh. "Do you want to be the same person you are now ten years from now? Do you want to be who you were in college? Changing and growing is one of the great things about life!"

Maria pondered her own words for a moment and was sobered by the thought that her days of personal growth had to be coming to an end.

John was still focusing on himself. "Fine," he said. Standing up, he readjusted the pillows in the chair before sitting back down. Maria waited while he fidgeted and got comfortable.

"Not long ago," Maria started when he had settled, "I read an interesting quote in a *Harvard Business Review* article entitled, 'Shakespeare's Characters Show Us How Personal Growth Should Happen.'"

John rolled his eyes. He felt like she was being patronizing when she started quoting the *Harvard Business Review*. Maria saw him roll his eyes but continued. He was still in defensive mode, and that was okay.

"The author, Declan Fitzsimons, states that Shakespeare's plays are riveting because he doesn't just let us get to know a static character. The characters go through tremendous change and personal development, and we get to watch."

Maria got more animated as she continued, "That's what I was talking about earlier! Tremendous change and personal development are interesting, exciting, and fun!"

John rolled his eyes again, but his interest had been piqued. Maria noticed the small shift in his attitude by the way his eyes focused on her after they rolled.

Maria continued, a little surprised at how accurately she remembered the article. "Fitzsimons wrote, 'Shakespeare teaches us moderns that in the face of an uncertain world, self-awareness—that much-vaunted leadership quality—is only worthy of the name when it is revelatory. And it can only be revelatory when we are willing to concede that we know ourselves only partially.'"

She ran inside to grab a pen and paper. John's only reaction was a raised eyebrow at his wife, but he didn't make a comment. Once she got back, she picked up where she left off.

As she drew on the paper, she said, "The Johari Window is a model that shows us what others know about us and what we do and don't know about ourselves." She finished triumphantly and showed John the box she had drawn.

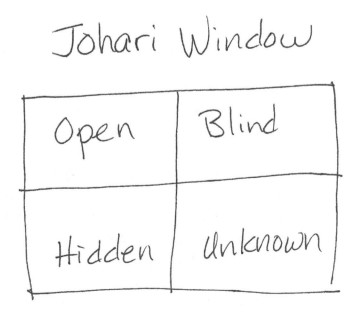

She pointed to the box with the pen and said, "Here is a Johari Window. It can help us better understand our relationship with others and ourselves."

Maria continued with her workshop speech, "Any information that I share with someone else is in the Open area." She circled the word *Open* and continued, "Once I let you know that I wear a size 8 shoe, it's in the Open region."

"Hidden items are things that I know, but no one else knows." She circled the word *Hidden* as she spoke. "We all have lots of those! We *should* have lots of them. We don't share everything." She paused to catch John's eye and said seriously, "It's really not a good idea to overshare." She thought that it was important for John to understand this part because he had a tendency to sometimes share bits of information that should be kept private.

She dropped her gaze, circled the word *Unknown,* and then continued, "Unknown items are things that I don't know about myself and no one else knows either. For example, maybe I could be a great computer programmer, and neither one of us knows it because I've never tried."

John was looking at the Johari Window that Maria had drawn, and she circled the word *Blind.* She went on, "The windowpane that's interesting is the Blind region. Those are things that other people know about us that we don't know about ourselves. Perhaps everyone else can see that I am inspirational, but I don't realize it. Maybe I have a distracting habit of messing with my hair that drives everyone crazy, and I don't even realize that I do it."

She could see that John was looking at her and counting the things that she did that he found annoying. Then she caught herself. *You are making an assumption*, she said to herself. *The only way to know what he is thinking is to ask.*

Then she decided that at that moment, she didn't want to hear a possible litany of complaints and get them off topic. She was in workshop teaching mode, not relationship-building mode.

So she continued, "It's important for all of us to know that we have items in the Blind region of our Johari Window. Some of them are good qualities, and some are not. Discovering those things about ourselves is revelatory! The new information can transform us. Like Shakespeare's characters, we don't remain static; we develop and grow. We are interesting!" She finished with a flourish of the pen in her hand.

Nonverbal Communication

John cocked an eyebrow and asked in an amused tone, "So what am I missing?"

Maria decided to be straightforward and said, "A lot of the nonverbal cues that people are sending you that would make your life and relationships much easier." She could see John shift into learning mode and sighed with relief.

"Okay, I'm listening," John said.

Maria started her lecture on nonverbal communication. "Back in 1972, Professor Albert Mehrabian said that our message is 7% words, 38% voice, and 55% body language." She said as an aside, "The only important thing to remember here is that our nonverbal communication has a huge influence on our message."

John acknowledged her words with a nod, and she went on, "Nonverbal communication includes facial expression, tone of voice, and body language. If I say 'I am so glad to be here' in a sarcastic tone while rolling my eyes and looking at my watch, you won't believe my words. That's so interesting!"

As she always did when delivering her workshops, Maria got genuinely excited the more she talked. "If the nonverbal and verbal messages are not the same, then we go with the nonverbal message. Our words have no meaning when the nonverbal message contradicts them!" she finished with her hands in the air.

John thought about the phrase "words have no meaning." That did explain some miscommunication between him and his coworkers. He'd said things to them but then they'd acted like he'd said something else.

Maria went on, "Of course, we want to be careful with the words that we use. However, we also need to pay close attention to our nonverbal messages. Crossed arms and stern looks can make us appear unapproachable or judgmental. If we deliver bad news while smiling, we send a very confusing message. It's important that we intentionally align our verbal and nonverbal messages."

John thought of work again. He'd said, "Good job!" to someone, but hadn't really thought they had been very thorough. The person had answered with a sarcastic, "Gee, thanks." John had been mystified at the time, but perhaps his nonverbal communication was indicating more of his own internal monologue than he thought. He tuned in once again as Maria continued.

"I've been talking about being aware of our own nonverbal communication, but we can learn a lot from watching the nonverbal signals that other people send us. If we watch people's nonverbal communication, we get clues to what they are thinking and how they are feeling," she explained.

She decided to move the conversation to the dinner with Russel and Tamara. "For example, Russel doesn't always say what's on his mind or tell anyone how he feels, but his nonverbal communication sometimes gives clues."

John brought his full attention back to Maria at the sound of Russel's name. "Sounds similar to a 'tell' in poker. Some movement or expression that lets the other players know that you are bluffing."

"Yes," said Maria. "It's very much like that. When Russel is uncomfortable or nervous, he fidgets with his watch band."

"Really?" John exclaimed, sounding surprised. "I never noticed that."

Maria kept herself from rolling her eyes as she went on. "When he is irritated or angry, he clenches his jaw and sometimes flares his nostrils out. It's very quick. You have to be paying attention to see it."

John was fully engaged now. He looked like an eager student ready to take notes. "Does Tamara have any tells?" he asked.

Maria considered his question for a moment and then said, "I haven't known her very long, but I have noticed that she laughs when she is nervous. Sometimes the laugh is out of place, but it's just because she's nervous."

"Good to know," John said. He did remember once when he'd felt insulted because he thought that Tamara was laughing at him.

Facts and Feelings

Maria added some more information. "It's important to know that every message has a fact and a feeling part. One must identify both parts in order to deal with a conflict effectively or to communicate clearly. When someone says 'Good morning!' or 'Pass the salt' or 'That doesn't make sense to me,' there is a feeling that goes along with the statement.

"We are humans, and humans have feelings," said Maria. "The only way to create lasting and meaningful relationships is to deal with both the fact and feeling parts of the conversations that we have with others."

She paused lecture mode and admitted with a rueful smile, "I learned this lesson late in life, and it would have saved me some time and trouble if I'd known about it sooner." Maria asked, "Do you remember the volunteer group that I led at the museum for a while?"

John nodded. He remembered that she came home from the meetings feeling frustrated.

Maria said, "During our monthly meetings, there was one young woman who always sat at my right hand and objected to everything that the group proposed. She objected on a factual level—logistics, budget, convenience. She slowed us down every single month." Maria relived a bit of the anger and frustration she had felt towards the woman, but took a deep breath and released it. She mentally chanted one of her mantras: *Keep the learning, not the story.* It helped her let go of the bad feelings attached to old mistakes.

She continued, "If I'd been savvier, I would have figured out that it wasn't the facts that she objected to. I had a vague notion that she was unhappy or resentful, but I had no idea why. There was a feeling component that I wasn't dealing with at that time. If I'd asked and listened, I could have saved us a lot of time arguing over facts for no good reason."

"What made you think she was unhappy?" John asked skeptically. "Maybe she simply needed all the facts laid out for her before she could get onboard."

"It was her nonverbals," Maria responded. "She always looked grumpy and put-upon. It may not have been anything that I was doing, but she was definitely unhappy about something.

"One of the most powerful things that you can do to build positive relationships is to pay attention to everyone's nonverbal communication and then ask about any telltale signs of an emotion. People often agree with something or say that everything is fine while their nonverbals say exactly the opposite."

Maria had seen the disconnect between verbal and nonverbal messages many times and could quickly come up with examples. She said, "Crossed arms, furrowed brows, and a lack of eye contact are all indicators that they don't agree, and not everything is fine. They will carry those unexpressed feelings out the door and stew in them if you don't bring them out in the open by asking some questions."

"I don't want to ask people how they feel!" John immediately said as he shook his head. "I don't want to deal with someone's emotions. What if they are angry? What if they are sad? What am I supposed to do about that?"

Personal Needs

"It can feel scary to voluntarily dive into the ocean of emotions," Maria answered calmly. "The water is murky and deep, and you have no idea what lurks down there. However, most people just want to be listened to and understood. Our personal needs are to be listened to, understood, and respected. You don't have to solve anyone's problems. Just meet their personal needs by listening attentively and respectfully."

John looked at her doubtfully, so Maria went on, "It does require a little bravery, but it is worth it. Naming an emotion that you see and asking about it can create an uncomfortable situation, but it isn't fatal. You generally get an explanation for the emotion that makes a lot of sense and gives you new information. The answers can be surprising—something that you wouldn't have guessed.

"I think that dinner with Russel and Tamara would be a good opportunity to practice noticing the tells and asking about emotions," said Maria.

"Like it wasn't already going to be hard enough to talk to those two without you there to run interference," John grumbled as he frowned.

Maria was surprised that he was aware of her running interference. She hadn't realized that he knew that she was managing conversations to keep the peace.

"Okay," said John with a deep breath. "I'll start." He turned to his wife to find her looking bemused. He smiled a little as he said, "You look surprised to hear that I was aware of you being the go-between for me and the kids."

His frankness startled her. "I am a little surprised. I didn't think that you were aware that I translated and kept the peace between you and the kids."

"I did realize it," he said in a matter-of-fact way. "And thank you. I appreciated it. Although it did let me get by without having to communicate on my own."

"Point taken," she said. "You are right. I robbed all of you of the chance to create a relationship on your own. I was afraid you might decide that you didn't like one another." She paused, thought about why, then admitted, "And that would have broken my heart."

John stood up and put his hands on her shoulders. He looked her in the eyes and sincerely said, "I'm sorry that I ever gave the impression that I might not like our children. I don't always understand them, but I do love them."

Maria took a deep breath and said, "Thank you. And now I know that you are going to have a great conversation with Russel and Tamara at dinner."

He smiled and said, "Me, too." It was a surprise to him that he really believed that.

Empathy

Maria shifted back into workshop mode. "You know," she said, "this is all a part of relationship awareness, which is a piece of emotional intelligence. You said that you didn't always understand the kids. The last piece of relationship awareness is being able to put yourself in their place and think how you would feel."

"You mean empathize," John said, smiling. He had listened to some of what she'd said over the years.

"Yes," she laughed, once again surprised at how much of her coachy mumbo jumbo John had heard and held on to. "I mean empathize. Thanks for translating. It's important to be able to imagine how other people might think and feel about something.

"In leadership workshops, we play a game that I call the 'Empathy Game.' It's a way to practice empathy for other people."

"I'm *game*," John said with a smirk, enjoying his own joke.

Maria rolled her eyes and smiled, then continued, "One of my participants gave us a great scenario. A delivery person brought them a sofa during our lunch break, and the delivery guy was super grumpy. So, we all came up with reasons why he might be grumpy.

"Can you think of any?" asked Maria.

"Sure," John said as he thought. "Maybe he'd had a fight with his wife that morning."

"That's a good story," Maria said encouragingly. "Can you think of another one?"

"Hmmm," John thought. "Perhaps he skipped lunch and had low blood sugar. Or maybe he'd just dropped something at the previous delivery and broken it."

"You are good at this!" Maria exclaimed happily. "There are a bunch of stories that we could make up. There is only one way to know the truth."

"What's that?" John asked.

Assumptions

"You ask," Maria said simply as she shrugged. "It seems sort of obvious when you think about it, but we don't often do it. We make up a story, decide that it is true, and move on. What we are really doing is making assumptions."

"So," John said, "I don't need to assume that Tamara is laughing at me when she laughs nervously."

"Exactly," Maria said, "The assumptions that we make up are just stories. We can only know what someone is thinking or feeling if we ask them."

Dinner with Russell

Russel and Tamara called John and said that they would come by and pick him up instead of meeting at the restaurant. It meant he had to clean up the public areas of the house in addition to himself, but he didn't mind. It felt good to get things back in order.

John thought he'd just be running out to the car when Russel showed up, but the doorbell rang a few minutes after he was done tidying up, surprising both him and Maria. He opened the door a crack and sure enough, both Russel and Tamara were standing at the door.

That's odd, John thought as he opened the door wider. Then he smiled, and they all stood looking at one another.

Russel said they were picking him up because parking was a problem at the restaurant they were going to. John was in investigative mode and immediately started looking for nonverbal clues about what was going on.

Sure enough, Russel was fidgeting with his watch band. Tamara laughed nervously and said, "Can we come in for a minute?"

John was sure something was up. He couldn't see Maria but was sure she was around. He wondered what she'd noticed so far.

Maria was indeed watching, but she hadn't noticed much more than John. She did think that Russel looked more serious than usual, maybe worried. He was definitely stressed. He wiped the palms of his hands on his pants before he shook his father's hand in greeting.

"Sure," said John, stepping away from the entry so they could come in. He was really glad that he'd cleaned the living room. He watched Russel and Tamara closely as they walked in. They were looking around apprehensively. Then they seemed to relax a bit when they saw the room was clean and orderly. Tamara laughed and said, "It looks really nice, John."

John got a little offended and said abruptly, "Did you think that it wouldn't?"

Russel stepped a bit in front of Tamara protectively. "Well, Dad, we weren't sure. Emmy said that you seem much better lately, but we wanted to check for ourselves." Russel looked his father in the eye and said, "We just want to be sure that you are okay. Mom used to say that the state of someone's living room is a good indicator of the state of their mind."

John did not remember Maria saying that, but Russel did always listen and pay attention. Then John decided to practice some empathy. If he was Russel and unsure of whether or not his father was still angry, drinking too much, and bathing too little, he'd be quite nervous too. He'd also be braced for another angry outbreak. John had yelled plenty in the aftermath of Maria's death.

It was touching that Russel and Tamara had braved the chance of an ugly scene to be sure that he was okay. John was suddenly very grateful for the love of these two young people in front of him.

John put his hand on Russel's shoulder and then pulled him into a hug. John couldn't see Russel's face but felt sure that it had a look of surprise on it. John said, "Thanks for checking on me. I appreciate it." He pulled away from Russel and put an arm around Tamara's shoulders and said, "I appreciate both of you."

Tamara looked up at him and said without any nervous laughter, "We both love you, John."

Russel had had his fill of emotions and said, "Let's go to dinner!"

John couldn't see Maria, but he felt sure that she was crying.

He was right. She was so full of happiness, gratitude and love that there just wasn't any room for the tears that spilled down her cheeks.

Your Turn

In Step 3, we are increasing our relationship awareness. This can only happen after we've increased our self-awareness.

Knowing how we are perceived by others increases both self-awareness and relationship awareness. Sometimes, how others react to us is obvious. Other times, it's more subtle. We can figure out how we impact others by paying attention to clues.

- **Johari Window.** By looking at the Johari Window, we can know that we have blind spots about ourselves. We should always be on the lookout for those blind spots. People do give us clues. If someone reacts in an unexpected way, they've probably interpreted what we said differently than we meant it. In this case, our impact is different from our intent. It's important to pause and ask some curious questions if you get an unexpected or mysterious response to something that you've said or done.

- **Nonverbal communication.** Paying attention to non-verbal communication can greatly enhance our aware-ness of how the people around us are feeling and how we are affecting them. Here are some tips for increas-ing our awareness of nonverbal communication.

    First, pay attention to your own nonverbals. Is your body language saying one thing while your words say something else? Make sure that your words and non-verbals are sending the same message.

Many of us are unaware of what our facial expressions look like. Stand in front of a mirror. Close your eyes and put a happy expression on your face. Open your eyes. Does your face look happy? Repeat the exercise for a resting expression, anger, and interest. Many people have a resting expression that looks angry or annoyed. You can change that habit and appear more approachable. (I worked on my resting facial expression in my 20s because people were always asking me if I was mad about something.)

Next, focus on the nonverbal messages that other people are sending you. Do they look nervous or uncomfortable? If so, ask them about it. Do they look happy? Comment on it, and get some details. Remember, we want to maintain a positivity ratio of at least 5:1.

- **Facts and feelings.** Every message has a fact and a feeling part. We must deal with both parts to resolve a situation or build a positive relationship. When someone is talking, pay attention to their verbal message, but also pay attention to the nonverbal signals that will tell you how they are feeling. You can make a comment like, "You sound really excited about this opportunity." Then let them decide if "excited" is the correct adjective. They will let you know if it's not, but at the very least, you've helped them define their feelings. You can accomplish the same thing by asking a question like, "How do you feel about that?" Obvious, but effective.

- **Personal needs.** Our personal needs are to be listened to, understood, and respected. When we meet people's personal needs, we increase the positivity of the relationship. Resist the urge to try to make people feel better if they are unhappy or angry. You are not responsible for their reactions and emotions. You can help just by listening attentively, which translates into meeting their personal needs.

- **Empathy.** Part of relationship awareness is putting ourselves in someone else's shoes and imagining how we would feel. Having empathy for someone is a hallmark of emotional intelligence.

  Practice empathy by imagining all the different reasons why a person might behave in a certain way. If the checkout person at the grocery store doesn't speak, think of all the different reasons why they might not be talking. Maybe their child is sick or they've had a fight with their significant other. Perhaps someone has gotten a worrisome medical test result.

  It's important to note that most of us are doing the best that we can and that most of us are facing some sort of challenge almost all of the time. Realizing that other people are coping in the best way that they know how can help us have empathy and understanding towards them.

- **Assumptions.** We make assumptions about all sorts of things. We assume that doors will open when we turn the knob and that Aunt Sally is always going to tell us her medical problems. Many of our assumptions are based on past experiences. However, we must be careful when making assumptions about other people and their motives. The Empathy Game can give us lots of possibilities, but asking is the only way to know for sure what is going on.

If you find yourself making up a story about someone's behavior, stop. Remember that it's a story in your head and the only way to know what a person is thinking and how they are feeling is to ask them.

Summary

There is a lot of noticing our internal dialogue in the exercises of Step 3 to increase our self-awareness. By paying attention to the feelings of others, we increase our relationship awareness.

- ✓ If you suspect that the impact you are having on a person or situation is different from your intent, stop and ask some curious questions about what the person is thinking and feeling.
- ✓ Ensure that your nonverbal communication matches your verbal message.
- ✓ Check your facial expressions in the mirror. (You may be surprised at your resting facial expression.) If you naturally look grumpy, you can intentionally change the way you hold your face.
- ✓ Always figure out both the fact and feeling parts of messages that people are sending.
- ✓ Meet people's personal needs to be listened to, understood, and respected. Making someone feel better is not your responsibility.

✓ Play the Empathy Game whenever you notice that you are making an assumption about why someone is acting a certain way.

STEP 4:
───── LISTEN MORE, ─────
TALK LESS

WHEN JOHN GOT BACK from dinner, he told Maria all about it. He had shared the things he'd been working on. He'd told them how work was going. They'd laughed about some old family memories.

"I did ask them how they felt about stuff," John said proudly. "Tamara likes their new neighbor, and Russel isn't thrilled with the latest Marvel movie."

"How is Russel's business doing?" Maria asked.

John thought for a minute and answered, "I don't know. He didn't say."

"Did Tamara get the job that she submitted a proposal for?" Maria asked, eagerly wanting to know about how their son and his girlfriend were doing.

John looked puzzled. "Why are you asking me those questions? How am I supposed to know that?" he asked, sounding a little irritated.

"By being fully present and asking questions," said Maria. She thought, *It's time for Step 4: 'Listen More, Talk Less.'*

Be Here Now

Maria looked at John and said, "You have made great progress! I don't want to take away from that. You had a nice dinner with Russel and Tamara where you enjoyed yourself. And it sounds like they did too."

John knew her and her coachy mumbo jumbo well enough to know there was more. "And?" he prompted as he plopped down on the sofa.

"And you can do even better! You can have conversations that are deeper and more meaningful." She sat in her favorite chair opposite him. "Let's work on Step 4, which is Listen More, Talk Less," she said. "It's a little more in-depth than it sounds."

"Good," John said with a wink and a smirk as he adjusted the pillows on the sofa. "I thought for a minute you were going to ask me to be a young lady."

The comment made Maria guffaw. He was referring to her story about being told to sit down and be quiet when she was a kid. It was nice that he had listened to it and remembered it. He was meeting her personal need to be listened to, understood, and respected. Awesome progress.

"No," she said still chuckling, "You don't have to sit quietly and look demure. The most important thing is to be fully present."

"I'm here," said John as he gestured to himself and the sofa. "What do you mean by 'fully present?'"

"Good point," Maria said. "I should have been more specific. It's important to be mentally present and notice the things that are happening in this moment. It's easy to daydream or start thinking of a response rather than just being mentally present and paying attention."

She waited for John's full attention and went on, "One of the greatest gifts that you can give someone is your time and undivided attention. One of my colleagues used to call and then not listen to what I said. She was talking to baristas or unpacking her briefcase. Her mind was not on our conversation. It felt demeaning—like I was not important enough to deserve her undivided attention."

"Yeah," John agreed. "I know what you mean. There is a woman at work who won't look up from her computer to answer a question. It's like she can't be bothered with someone as trivial as me."

"Exactly," Maria said. "Sometimes, people aren't doing something else, but you can tell that they are thinking about something else. Maybe they are considering their response to what you are saying or maybe they are just thinking about what they want to have for dinner. There is no way to know where their mind is, but we know it isn't here and focused on us.

"We want to be sure that we don't do any of those things. We want to be fully present, listening attentively and paying attention to any nonverbal clues that are present."

"I did stay present most of the time during dinner with Russel and Tamara. I might have been thinking about what I was going to say next a few times," John admitted.

"That's totally normal," Maria assured him. "Paying attention completely takes some practice, and none of us can do it all the time."

Sending Solutions

"We also have a tendency to want to solve people's problems for them," Maria continued. "We want to help. Once someone tells us about their challenges, we want to give them back a solution. It's another normal reaction that isn't always that helpful."

"How can helping someone solve a problem not be helpful?" John asked, genuinely confused.

Maria answered, "There is a difference between sending a solution that would work for us and helping someone solve a problem. One way, we are telling them what to do. The other way, we are collaborating and brainstorming together."

"Like my conversation with George about the project!" said John, experiencing a light-bulb moment.

"Yes," Maria said with a satisfied smile, "exactly like that."

She continued, "Let me give you another example. I had a client whose family was getting annoyed with him. When they would tell him about things that were going on in their lives, he would immediately start to send them solutions."

As an aside, she said, "Honestly, most of the time we just want to be listened to. Remember that our personal needs are to be listened to, understood, and respected.

"Anyway," she continued with her story, "I told him to try asking three questions before he sent any solutions. That was it. Just ask three questions first."

"What happened?" John asked, curious about the outcome.

"At the beginning of our next coaching call, he said, 'My wife said to tell you that she loves you,'" Maria answered and then laughed thinking about it. It was a great moment for a life coach.

She went on to clarify, "It's best if the questions cannot be answered with a yes or a no. Those are called open-ended questions, and they get the person asked to think about their answer."

"Can you give me some examples?" John asked.

"Of course!" said Maria. "Since we always want to figure out both the fact and feeling parts of a message, a good start is: How do you feel about that?"

John thought for a moment and said, "Yes, I can see how that would get me to pause and think for a minute."

"A good follow-up question is: What about it makes you feel that way?" said Maria.

"So, by asking the questions," said John, "you are helping the person analyze their own problem."

"Exactly!" Maria said happily, emphasizing her excitement with a clap. John really was catching on to this stuff quickly. Maybe some of the things she'd said over the years really had been sinking in without her knowing it.

"Got any more examples?" he asked, giving her his undivided attention.

Maria paused to think about her list of coaching questions. "Another good one is: If it turned out perfect, what would it look like?" John nodded his head in understanding, so she continued, "Most questions that start with 'what' are good ones."

She rambled off a few more questions. "What is the hardest part about this? What would be the easiest thing to change? What part of this is in your control? What concerns you the most? What do you like best?"

She paused for a moment and said, "Not sending solutions or making suggestions is harder than it sounds. In workshops, I have the participants practice coaching each other on real-life topics. I give the people being coached an index card and have them write *telling* on one end of it. Whenever the person coaching starts to *tell* rather than *ask*, they hold up the card.

"I know from watching this exercise for more than a decade that it's way more difficult to ask than tell," she continued. "The telling cards get flashed pretty often. The people who are coaching struggle to come up with open-ended questions and often end up telling the other person what they need to do to solve the issue."

John sighed and said, "I guess that anything worth mastering takes practice." He was thinking of his current exercise and running regimen. That was also taking a lot of work and practice.

"Yes," Maria agreed. "You can't get good at anything unless you work at it.

"When asking those questions, it's important to do it with genuine curiosity. We can all tell when someone is faking interest. It feels very patronizing. Asking the three questions shouldn't feel like checking boxes off a to-do list.

"And," she said, "our questions don't have to be about problems. By asking people questions about what interests them, I've learned about knitting, drawing, orchid care, football, cooking techniques, technological gadgets, and tires—just to name a few topics. What people know is amazing! And asking people about what interests them is a great way to develop and enhance the positivity of our relationships with them."

John sat with this information and thought for a minute. "That's why people were drawn to you. You didn't talk about you; you let them talk about themselves!"

Maria laughed and said, "Right! And you don't have to worry about what to say or how to sound smart. You just ask a lot of curious questions, and people think you are brilliant." She paused and said, "There is a study about that."

John smiled and said, "I'm sure that there is."

Then he jumped up off the sofa and said, "I'm going to try out Step 4 tomorrow! I'm having lunch with Antonio. We always get along, but now that I'm thinking about all of this, I feel that our conversations are . . ." And he trailed off.

Maria let him decide on the word that he was looking for, but she was pretty sure he was going to say . . .

"Superficial," John said.

It was exactly the word that Maria had been thinking. John and Antonio's conversations were generally lively and fun, but they didn't talk about what was bothering them or how they felt about things. She was genuinely excited about the possibilities for their relationship.

Lunch with Antonio

John walked into the restaurant and saw Antonio at the table. He was reading something on his phone, his sandy hair slicked back so it wasn't falling into his face like it usually did. John took note of his nonverbals. Antonio looked concerned. Maybe a little angry. Antonio took a breath, looked up at the sky, looked back down at his phone, and stabbed a rapid response into the phone.

John waited until Antonio had finished sending the message before he approached. When Antonio saw him, his entire demeanor changed. Antonio stood up and smiled, all traces of previous anxiety gone. He was laughing a bit and said, "Hey, Dad!" Antonio gave John a good man hug—a hug face-to-face with their hips side to side.

John had never noticed before that they didn't just stand toe-to-toe and give each other a hug. When he thought of Antonio's immediate change in mood and facial expression, John realized that Antonio had put his game face on. John thought, *He's not going to show how he really feels.*

They sat down and ordered. John asked Antonio how things were going. Antonio immediately answered that everything was great and started talking about a movie he'd just seen. The conversation rolled between internet memes, movies, and a few family jokes and memories.

John realized that the conversation wasn't going to go any deeper unless he did something. He took a breath and said, "I noticed when I walked in that you looked like something on your phone was irritating you. What was it?" The direct question was a gamble, but John had decided to take it.

Antonio paused for a moment. John thought that perhaps he was considering which answer to give—the usual "everything is awesome" statement or the truth. Antonio sighed and said, "Sanya and I are arguing about whether or not to start a family." He rubbed a hand down his face before continuing, "I want to start now, but Sanya wants to wait until we've saved enough money for a down payment on a house."

"That's a tough situation," John sympathized. Antonio looked downcast as he absentmindedly played with his napkin. John was tempted to share a similar situation that he and Maria had been through but remembered the three-question rule. He remembered the first question that Maria recommended and continued, "How do you feel about that?"

Antonio looked up. He was a little surprised at being asked a serious question by his father. John wasn't sure that Antonio was going to respond, but chose to give him time to think about his answer.

They sat silent for a moment before Antonio sighed and then said, "I understand her desire to get a house, so we have a safe and comfortable place to raise a family. Babies are expensive, and once we have one, it will be harder to save."

John decided to use one of Maria's questions and said, "What is the hardest part about this?"

Antonio answered quickly, "It's that Sanya and I both want the same things: a family and a house. We are only arguing about the order, but it's driving us apart."

John was genuinely curious at this point. He wanted to ask how much they'd saved and if they knew the price range of houses, but those were steps to creating and sending a solution. He needed one more really curious question.

"What are you afraid of?" he asked his son.

Antonio sighed and answered, "That we will never have enough money for a down payment or that we'll be too old to have kids once we can afford a house."

"What do you think Sanya is afraid of?" John asked him gently, happy that his son was opening up to him.

"I think she's afraid that if we start a family, we will be stuck living in an apartment forever. She hates living in a box surrounded by other people," Antonio said sadly.

John had a bunch of budgeting suggestions in his head that he really wanted to share. He sincerely wanted to help, but he held himself back because he knew his son would benefit from coming to the conclusion on his own. So, he said, "It sounds like you are both worried about being stuck forever in one place or another. What would help you both feel better about the choices you are facing?"

Antonio thought hard for a minute or two. It was difficult, but John stayed silent and let him think. "You know," Antonio said, "I think a definite timeline would help us both, but to do that we need some hard data. For example, how much does a house that we want cost? Do we wait until we can afford our dream house or can we begin with a starter house? Do we really have to have 20% for the down payment? What is the latest date that we are comfortable starting a family?" The solutions spilled out of Antonio one by one. The more he talked, the more enthusiastic he sounded. His entire demeanor had changed, and he looked hopeful.

"Those are really great questions to discuss with Sanya!" John exclaimed, a large smile on his face. He was astonished at how well the conversation was going. He was helping by asking questions.

They talked some more and, when lunch was over, Antonio jumped to his feet.

"Thanks, Dad!" he said as he hugged his father once again, this time a little tighter. "I'm going to go speak with Sanya." He turned to go but then turned back and said, "Don't take this the wrong way, but that felt a lot like talking with Mom. I would usually have a clearer picture of what was going on after I spoke with her, and I've missed that."

John smiled and said, "High praise. Thanks, Antonio. I love you."

Antonio smiled and said, "I love you too, Dad." Then he turned and bounded out of the restaurant. John looked forward to reporting to Maria about their conversation. He hoped that she was still here.

Your Turn

Many of us have a tendency to tell other people how to solve their problems or to share when something similar happened to us. However, we create more positivity in our relationships when we resist the urge to "tell," and instead ask curious questions.

- **Be here now.** When speaking with someone, practice being fully present. At least once a day, focus completely on what someone is telling you. Remember, we want to meet people's personal needs to be listened to, understood, and respected. People don't feel respected when they get the impression that we have other things that we'd rather be doing.

- **Sending solutions.** Before making any suggestions when someone shares a problem or challenge, ask three questions first. Try to use curious questions—ones that can't be answered with yes or no. We build the positivity of a relationship by asking nonjudgmental questions and listening intently to the answers.

  Asking curious questions is a great way to get to know people. If you find yourself with a group of people that you don't know, start asking questions. You can begin with the obvious ones like, "What do you do?" Then, ask about how they spend their free time or what is their favorite thing to do on the weekend. Then deep dive from there. Remember to ask about facts and feelings.

  Silence is okay. Don't rush to fill a silence. Give people time to think about your question and their answer.

Summary

We increase our relationship awareness by being fully present, asking curious questions, and paying close attention to the answers (which allows us to ask more curious questions!).

- ✓ When someone is speaking with you, be fully present in mind and body.
- ✓ Ask three questions before making any suggestions.
- ✓ Get to know others by asking curious questions.
- ✓ Silence is good. Don't rush to fill a silent moment.

STEP 5:
———— CREATE A PEACEFUL ————
FOUNDATION

MARIA WAS THERE when John got home, and he regaled her with the details of his lunch with Antonio. He was so excited about how well the conversation had gone that he'd started talking before she even asked. He was proud of himself, and Maria was proud of him too. He'd done a great job. She was also immensely grateful that John was stepping up to have the conversations that she had facilitated for him and the children in the past.

"I feel so good!" John exclaimed, a wide smile lighting up his face. "I'm not sure why, but I feel great!"

Maria looked at him with a proud smile and thought, *What a perfect segue to Step 5—and maybe the end.*

"That is great. I am so proud of you." Her voice matched his enthusiasm. Then she added, "And I know why you feel so great."

Outward Focus

John looked at her like she held the secrets of the universe and said, "Really! Tell me. I want to feel this way all the time!"

Maria laughed, her heart feeling full and warm. "I'm not sure anyone can create that feeling all the time, but we can at least make it a regular thing. It's time for Step 5: Create a Peaceful Foundation."

John sobered a bit, his smile falling slightly. "The last step?" he asked. He was a little apprehensive about finishing, unsure of what would happen next. The unknown was a scary thing. He'd gotten used to having his hallucination around, although he didn't really think about her as a hallucination anymore.

"Yep," she said with the best smile she could muster as she led him to the living room. "You have come so far, and there is only one step left. Step 5 is 'Creating a Peaceful Foundation,' and one piece of that is being helpful, but not necessarily in the 'doing' sense of being helpful."

"What do you mean?" John asked as he got comfy on the sofa.

Maria noticed that there wasn't any defensiveness in his question. It was just an awesome curious question. It made her happy to see how far John had come in such a short time. He was actually the best coaching client she'd ever had because he was open-minded, positive, and diligent about implementing the concepts he learned. She answered, "What's most important is the mindset that we have."

She went on, "When we have an inward mindset, we focus on ourselves. We notice how we feel and what's going wrong. We analyze what we've said and what others have said to us. It's a small world that generally does not lead to much happiness."

John interrupted with a question, "But isn't that what we were doing when we were talking about self-awareness?"

"Good point," Maria said. She thought for a moment. It really was a good catch on John's part. She answered, "To me, it's the difference between checking in on ourselves and a situation, and dwelling only on ourselves and the situation. The former is raising our awareness, and the latter is a bit of an obsession with ourselves to the exclusion of considering anyone else."

"That makes sense," John said as he nodded his head in understanding. "I see the difference."

Maria continued, "We broaden our world when we have an outward mindset. We use empathy to guess how others might feel and react. We take others' needs and wants into consideration. We see places and times when we could make a difference in a positive way." She stopped, took a breath, and went on, "And research shows that we are happier and live longer when we help others." She shrugged and said, "It sounds counterintuitive, but we create more happiness for ourselves when we focus on what we can do for others."

John asked, "Are you suggesting that I give away all my belongings and devote my life to helping others?"

Maria laughed and said, "Only if you want to!"

John smiled back and asked, "What do you mean?"

"Of course, we always have to consider what is best for us in any situation, and boundaries are a good thing. As I said in the beginning, it's more of how we see and think about the world than what we actually do. When we see a need that we can reasonably meet and follow through with it, we feel good about ourselves and the world."

"After my conversation with Antonio," said John, "I can see that asking questions is a good way to help people."

"Right!" Maria exclaimed. "And you asked those questions because your focus was on Antonio. You weren't thinking about yourself."

"True," John said. "I wasn't thinking about myself or what I wanted to say next or worrying about looking stupid."

"Exactly. You were operating with an outward mindset."

"Helping the kids is easy because they want a relationship with me," John added, looking deep in thought. He was thinking about a few people at work and said, "Not everyone wants my help. Some people don't want a relationship with me at all."

"That's true and an important thing to be aware of," Maria answered. "For a relationship to be healthy, both parties have to care about each other and about the health of the relationship."

Relationship Entity

Maria stood up from the couch and walked to the desk in the bedroom for a pen and paper. She came back and settled down next to John on the sofa, ready to draw again. "In systems coaching, we think of the relationship between two or more people as a living, breathing entity." She drew it on the piece of paper as John looked on, interested.

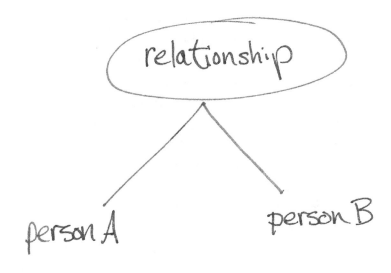

"In a healthy relationship, Person A cares about their own concerns, but Person B's concerns also matter, as do the needs of the relationship. Person B must feel the same about themselves, Person A, and the relationship," Maria said.

She continued, "If one person in a relationship cares only about themselves and not the other person or the relationship with coworkers that they create together, then the relationship is not a healthy one. It's important to recognize when someone is only out for themselves and do what you can to protect yourself."

When John acknowledged what she said, she added, "At work, we must maintain a professional, courteous relationship and we can do our best to be helpful and care about them, but it's never going to be a reciprocal, nurturing relationship unless that person changes their mindset."

Maria had answered John's question about his coworkers, and he said, "It will make it easier to deal with a couple of people at work when I just accept that they don't want a relationship."

Maria nodded her head, then continued. "There is a concept from the book *Triggers* by Marshall Goldsmith that has been helpful to me and others. He talks about accepting people as they are. He says that the chair is a chair, meaning people rarely change. If someone is annoying and continually does something annoying, it's best just to accept that it's always going to be that way and not spend any Emotional Pennies on it. The chair isn't suddenly going to change into a chaise lounge or a sofa."

"And *that* makes it even easier," John said, pointing at Maria for emphasis.

Maria interjected, "Remember, you don't get to abuse the chair by jumping up and down on the cushions. This mindset is all about acceptance of the chair as it is."

John thought for a minute and added, "It reminds me of imagining everyone looking out through their own Frame of Reference. It's easier to accept them and their opinions if I realize their values, priorities, experiences, and beliefs are different from mine."

"Excellent!" Maria said happily. "You really have mastered all the material that we have covered."

Cancel That Order!

John smiled at Maria's comment before pausing to evaluate himself and his progress. He admitted, "I do still worry about things. I have trouble sleeping sometimes. I mean, everything that we've talked about is helpful, but my mind still jumps on the hamster wheel sometimes and won't stop."

"The first thing to try," Maria said, "is a method that I call 'Cancel that Order!' I don't know if you remember that I used to be a huge worrier."

John did remember her worrying a lot when the kids were little. He hadn't really noticed that she'd stopped but couldn't think of a time recently when she'd seemed overly worried about anything.

When John didn't say anything, she continued, "I realized a couple of things. First, worrying about what may or may not happen is a huge emotional energy drain. It costs a lot of Emotional Pennies. Second, my worrying did not improve anyone's chances of success or survival."

She went on, "As I began studying human behavior, I learned that worrying and negative self-talk are habits just like any other habit. We can change them with some effort. I designed a mental game to help me change my worrying ways."

John was listening closely, so she continued, "I pretended that every thought was a request for something that I wanted. When I thought about something, I was placing an order for it with the Universe. When I thought, 'I am not going to have enough money this month,' I was placing an order for that to happen. Immediately, I would think or say out loud, 'Cancel that order!' Then I would replace the order with a new one: 'I have plenty of money to make it through the month.'"

As an aside, she said, "It's simply creating new thought habits and intentionally changing the way we think. It's very powerful."

John said excitedly, "We are saving Emotional Pennies by waving around the Magic Wand of Destiny—making intentional choices about our thoughts!"

Maria was so proud of John that she felt she would burst. The information that they'd discussed was a part of who he was now. He could recall it and use it appropriately. She'd never had a better student.

She smiled at him and said, "Exactly. Very impressive."

Then she continued, "I actually clap my hands together and say 'Cancel that order!' with some enthusiasm when I am canceling an order. Then I replace the negative thought with a thought about something that I want to happen or with an affirmation. Creating a positive internal dialogue makes life way less stressful."

She decided to share the other circumstances when the exercise was useful. She continued, "'Cancel that order!' is also very effective in dealing with negative self-talk. Pay attention to your thoughts. Any time you hear yourself thinking that you aren't enough in some way, cancel that order! If you walk to the closet thinking, 'I don't look good in any of my pants,' cancel that order! Replace it with what you want: 'I look good in anything I put on.'"

John looked thoughtful and said, "I can see how changing my thought patterns could really help to lower my stress level—and make me feel less anxious."

"It can do both of those things," Maria said. Then she added, "Changing our thoughts can't magically change our reality. However, our reality will never change until we change our thoughts and beliefs. 'Cancel that order!' is the first step in creating the life and environment that you desire."

She stopped to think for a moment and decided to share one of her personal methods for dealing with worries. "I have one more method that might be helpful. Would you like to hear about it?" She looked at John expectantly.

"Why not?" John said with a smile. "Everything you've talked about so far has been really useful."

Two Bins

"When I find myself dwelling on a situation, I ask myself which bin it belongs in," Maria said.

John was intrigued and had grown to like all her coachy mumbo jumbo. "What do you mean?" he asked.

"I visualize two bins," Maria said. "One is a normal-looking office trash can that you might toss a ball of paper into. That bin is mine. The other is a very shiny, galvanized steel trash bin with a lid. That one belongs to God—or whatever higher power you believe in. You can also think of it as the

Universe's bin." She knew that John had a tenuous relationship with organized religion.

"When I find myself thinking about something," she went on, "I ask myself, '*Whose problem is this?*' If I can do something about it, it's mine. If I have the power to improve the situation in some way with my actions, it belongs to me and goes in my bin."

"What sorts of things go in your bin?" John asked.

"Maybe I've had a misunderstanding with someone. I can talk with them about it. Maybe I've gained a little weight that makes me uncomfortable. I can move more and eat healthier for a while." She sincerely wished that she'd consciously put her heart palpitations in her own bin and done something like having them checked out. By not making an intentional choice, she'd put the situation in God's bin.

"If it's something that I have no control over, it goes in God's bin. I lift the lid a bit, toss the situation in, and slam the lid back down." She smiled wryly and said in a whisper, "They try to get out and come back to me."

John laughed at the picture in his head that Maria had described. He could visualize Maria stuffing something in the shiny, silver trash can and slamming down the lid with a triumphant look on her face.

Before he could ask for examples, she added, "Worries about the kids driving around at night go in God's bin. I've done what I can to teach them safe driving techniques and good judgment, but when they are actually out there in the world, there is nothing that I can do. Their safety goes into God's bin." She smiled sheepishly and said, "I usually say a little prayer when I put things in God's bin."

John thought of things that were keeping him up at night. Some were work situations that he could do something about. Some were worries about money and the future. Sorting them into the two bins could help. He could clearly see which things he could change or influence and which ones were completely beyond his control.

He stood up and took Maria's hands in his, pulling her to her feet too. "Thanks, Hallucination," he said. "I am so much happier than I was when you first showed up. It doesn't feel like the changes were big, but my relationships are more positive, my health is better, and my job is secure. I really do appreciate everything that you've taught me."

He gave Maria a warm and sincere hug. She was flattered and joyful. She had a really good feeling about her family. She knew that they would all be okay without her.

When she pulled away, she said, "You have made big changes and done some hard work. Don't shortchange yourself on the amount of commitment you've shown. The transformation in you is truly remarkable."

John started for the kitchen, then turned around and said, "When you first appeared and told me that I could stop being angry all the time, I didn't believe you. I didn't see how it could be possible."

He smiled, put his arms out to the side, and twirled around. "But I am not angry now! I'm positive and hopeful. I have good relationships with the kids, their partners, and even the grandkids." He turned to make his way back toward the kitchen but stopped again, turned around, blew her a kiss, then turned back to the kitchen as he called out, "Good night, Hallucination!"

When he reached the kitchen door, he turned one last time and Maria saw that he was a little choked up. He said, "I am very, very grateful for the time that we've spent together and the help that you've given me."

He didn't say it, but Maria felt that he now had a proper sense of closure around her death.

Your Turn

In Step 5, we learned the importance of maintaining a positive frame of mind and read about some tools that can help us stay open and optimistic.

- **Outward focus.** One of the best and easiest ways to foster our own happiness is to help others. We can take actions to help them, and we can help by meeting their personal needs to be listened to, understood, and respected. By turning our focus outward instead of inward, we see how we can help others and connect with them more effectively.

    It's easier to have an outward mindset and help others if we are in a positive mental state. In technical terms, when we create an expansive, joyful feeling, we are in an autonomic nervous system state called the ventral vagal state. The official term isn't that important, but getting into the ventral vagal state and staying there as much as possible is.

    When we are in the ventral vagal state, we are more open-minded, creative, and better at seeing the big picture. To be a great leader and create positive relationships, we must be in the ventral vagal state. Abilities like problem-solving and showing patience are biologically unavailable to us when we are in one of the other two states: sympathetic nervous system state and dorsal vagal state.

    When we are in "fight or flight," we are in the sympathetic nervous system state, and we are on high alert for things that go wrong. It's a high-energy and high-anxiety state.

When we are in the dorsal vagal state, we feel hopeless and depressed. It is a very low-energy, lethargic state.

There are lots of tools and techniques that can help us stay in the ventral vagal state. Here is a list of things to try. It isn't a complete list, but it will give you a good place to start.

→ *Your own happy place:* Visualize a real or imagined situation that makes you feel expansive and content.

→ *Positivity portfolio*: Create a book or photo album full of images that make you feel joyful.

→ *Breathing techniques:* Try intentional rhythmic breathing.

→ *Mindfulness:* Be fully present in the moment and pay attention to nothing else.

→ *Meditation:* Practice this form of mindfulness when you sit quietly.

→ *Success journal:* Keep a list of your successes that you can look back on when you are feeling low.

→ *Sound/music:* Listening to music or other soothing sounds and singing can make us feel better.

→ *Art:* Get engrossed in a creative process.

→ *Uplifting books, movies, shows, and podcasts:* These can distract us and give us new perspectives.

→ *Gratitude journal:* This is a very powerful way to create an attitude of gratitude.

→ *Exercise/movement:* Any movement is good, and walking for 30 minutes a day can have a positive impact on our mental health.

→ *Emotional freedom technique (Tapping):* Some people love this technique and enjoy great results. You can find a lot of information about it online.

→ *Nature:* Studies show that we are relaxed and rejuvenated when we get out in nature.

→ *Sleep:* Many of us don't get enough sleep to function at our best.

→ *Connection:* It is impossible to sustain the ventral vagal state without nurturing, reciprocal relationships.

You can find more information online about every item on the list.

• **Relationship entity.** When creating positive relationships, you need to think of them as living entities that need care and attention. Relationship entities can include two or more people. A marriage has a relationship entity, and a team at work has a relationship entity.

A relationship between two or more people cannot thrive unless everyone in that relationship cares about everyone else and the health of the relationship itself. You can maintain a relationship with people who don't care about your needs or the relationship, but it won't be a positive, thriving relationship.

Sometimes, we need to maintain relationships that aren't what we would define as healthy. Those are often work relationships. In that case, it's important to remember that the person is probably not going to change, and it's best to accept them as they are. It will save you a lot of Emotional Pennies. As Marshall Goldsmith says, "The chair is a chair."

It can also help to remind ourselves that everyone looks at the world through a different Frame of Reference, and we have no idea of the experiences that have shaped a person's worldview.

Analyze your important relationships. Are they healthy and positive? Does everyone in the relationship care about the needs of the others and the health of the relationship itself?

Practice accepting people that you find irritating or annoying. Remember that they will probably not change, and you are just tossing Emotional Pennies into a chair that will probably always be that same chair. It is a waste of Emotional Pennies (not to mention a waste of your time) to try and change someone.

- **Cancel that Order!** Habitual negative thinking is another Emotional Penny consumer. Thought patterns are habits that can be changed with some intentional practice. "Cancel that Order!" is a great way to change some thought habits.

  Pretend that every thought is a request to the Universe. When a negative thought pops up, say "Cancel that Order!" either aloud or in your mind. You can clap your hands for emphasis. Then intentionally think of something that you do want. Keep repeating it until your mind is ready to move on to something else.

  Worry can also use up a lot of Emotional Pennies. We want to do something about the things we can influence, and we want to let go of the things that we cannot.

- **Two bins.** Imagine two bins or trash cans. You can visualize them in any way that you want. One bin is yours. The other belongs to a higher power. Pick the higher power that has meaning for you.

  When you find yourself worrying about something, ask yourself if it belongs to you or your higher power. If it's yours, make a plan. Figure out what you can do to influence the situation in a positive way. It goes in your bin.

  If you have no control over the situation, put it in your higher power's bin, and slam the lid down on it. Any time that worry creeps back, firmly place it in the correct bin. Worrying about something that you can't influence or control is a huge waste of Emotional Pennies.

Summary

Step 5 is about creating a firm and peaceful foundation from which to live your life. You can only be creative, stay disciplined, and be open-minded if you are in the ventral vagal state. The exercises in this step will help you get to and stay in that relaxed and open state.

- ✓ We feel happier and lighter when we enthusiastically help others. Maintain an outward focus by paying attention to the verbal and nonverbal cues of those around you. Does someone seem lost or overwhelmed? You can help by both taking action and by asking curious questions. Sometimes the best help we can offer is meeting someone's personal needs to be listened to, understood, and respected.

✓ Pick one or two of the items listed above that will help you achieve and maintain the ventral vagal state and give them a try. We can only be open-minded and creative when we are in the ventral vagal state.

✓ Analyze your important relationships. Are they healthy and positive? Does everyone in the relationship care about the needs of the others and the health of the relationship itself?

   If it's a personal relationship, it's important to talk to the other person or people and share your concerns. Some personal relationships are not salvageable.

   If it's a professional relationship, it's important to always behave in a kind and calm manner. However, it may never be a nurturing and reciprocal relationship. That's okay! Just stay professional in your behavior.

✓ Practice accepting people that you find irritating or annoying. Remember that they will probably not change, and you are just tossing Emotional Pennies into a chair that will probably always be that same chair. It is a waste of Emotional Pennies (not to mention a waste of your time) to try and change someone.

✓ When a negative or unhelpful thought pops into your head, practice *Cancel that Order!* Clap your hands and say it out loud! Then replace that thought with a useful, empowering one.

✓ We don't have control over all the events in the world. It can be helpful to separate the things that we can influence and change from the things that we cannot. Put your responsibilities in your bin and put the rest in your higher power's bin. Worrying about things you cannot control does not help the situation.

THE STORY ENDS

MARIA SAT IN THE LIVING ROOM for a while, long after John had gone to bed. Since her death she had been able to sleep or zone out at night, but she felt different this evening. She was feeling lighter, less solid. She could hear John snoring softly across the hallway, so she decided to go into his room. Once there, she stood watching him sleep for a minute and then thought of the kids.

She had tried visiting other people, but her children were the only ones that could draw her presence. She closed her eyes and thought of Emmy, the fierce and loving mother and wife. She opened her eyes and was next to Emmy's bed. She and Ian were asleep, just like the last time she was here.

Emmy looked so young this evening. Maria felt that she had softened a bit because John had started taking some of the responsibility for the family. Emmy didn't feel like everything was on her shoulders anymore, and she'd become a little more patient with everyone. Her sense of humor came out more often. The changes in John had given Emmy room to make some changes of her own.

She walked into her grandchildren's room next. She was profoundly sad that she couldn't be a part of their lives. She loved playing with them and reading to them. Then she remembered that John had taken on those activities, and she was grateful to him for that.

Then she closed her eyes and thought of Antonio. She saw his light-hearted exterior and the intense heart that hid within. She opened her eyes and was next to Antonio's bed. He and Sanya were asleep. They had made a two-year plan that included both a house and a baby. John had helped them get through a rough patch.

Next, she thought about Russel, her youngest and most serious child. She opened her eyes and was standing next to his bed. He and Tamara were asleep. From John, she knew that Russel's business was doing well. Russel had told John that he was shopping for an engagement ring. There was a lot of joy coming in to the family.

Then she thought of John in the way that she had for most of her after-death time when she wanted to go to him. She thought of the grumpy and angry guy that he had turned into over the years.

She opened her eyes only to find that she was still standing by Russel's bed. She was confused for a moment, wondering why she hadn't traveled to John. Then it hit her. John was truly not that person anymore.

She closed her eyes once again and thought of him as he was now. Now he is kind and generous. He has a positive, outward mindset. He has strong relationships with his peers, friends, and family.

She opened her eyes and was delighted to be standing next to John's bed. He was still asleep. She bent down, kissed him on the forehead, and said, "Goodbye, John." He stirred a bit and murmured, "Goodbye, Maria." Then he was breathing deeply again.

She couldn't recall him ever calling her Maria since her death. He'd always called her Hallucination. She sat down in her favorite chair and felt waves of profound joy and gratitude. She couldn't begin to express how much she appreciated this second chance to help her family and say a proper goodbye.

As she sat there, she began to feel less present. It was like her body was slowly dissolving into light and her spirit felt stronger. Overwhelming peace engulfed her, and she knew that everyone was going to be fine.

Yes, everything was going to be fine.

It was time to go on.

ABOUT THE AUTHOR

As a leadership coach, trainer, and speaker, KATHY STODDARD TORREY has been helping individuals and organizations achieve success by creating positive relationships for more than 20 years. She has provided leadership and interpersonal communication seminars internationally to leaders in a variety of industries and to companies such as Deutsche Bank and GE Aviation. She has a Bachelor of Journalism and a Master's Degree in Business Administration from the University of Texas at Austin.

People who work with Kathy gain enhanced communication skills, improved self-awareness, better stress management, and the ability to deal with conflicts confidently and positively. These qualities and abilities create leaders who can inspire, motivate, and influence others.

Organizations with high emotional intelligence have higher productivity, improved employee morale, lower turnover, adaptability in the face of change, and higher customer satisfaction.

Go to *KathyStoddardTorrey.com* to see how you can work with Kathy to improve your emotional intelligence or the emotional intelligence of your organization. She offers keynote speeches, workshops, in-depth training programs, and coaching for individuals, groups, and teams.

Download Kathy's Checklist

 Go to *https://checklist.kathystoddardtorrey.com* to download a checklist with all the exercises in *Elevate Your Emotional Intelligence*.

Printed in the USA
CPSIA information can be obtained
at www.ICGtesting.com
CBHW030034240324
5636CB00005B/6

9 798990 182608